Digital Governance in Municipalities Worldwide (2015-16)

Seventh Global E-Governance Survey: A Longitudinal Assessment of Municipal Websites Throughout the World

Marc Holzer, Ph.D.

University Professor, School of Public Affairs and Administration
Director, The E-Governance Institute,
The National Center for Public Performance
Rutgers, The State University of New Jersey, Campus at Newark

Aroon P. Manoharan, Ph.D.

Associate Director, The E-Governance Institute
Associate Professor and Director
Global Comparative Public Administration MPA Program
Department of Public Policy and Public Affairs
John W. McCormack Graduate School of Policy and Global Studies
University of Massachusetts Boston

Senior Research Associate

Alex Ingrams, Ph.D. Student, Rutgers University-Newark

Research Associates

Dongyoen Kang, Ph.D. Student, Rutgers University-Newark
Sean Mossey, Ph.D. Student, University of Massachusetts Boston
Chengxin Xu, Ph.D. Student, Rutgers University-Newark

Digital Governance in Municipalities Worldwide (2015-16)
Seventh Global E-Governance Survey:
A Longitudinal Assessment of Municipal Websites Throughout the World
©2016 National Center for Public Performance

E-Governance Institute
National Center for Public Performance
Rutgers University, Campus at Newark

111 Washington Street
Newark, New Jersey 07102
Tel: 973-353-5093 | Fax: 973-353-5097
www.ncpp.us

Printed in the United States of America
ISBN 13: 978-1537555966
ISBN 10: 1537555960

Contents

Acknowledgements

This volume, *Digital Governance in Municipalities Worldwide 2015-16,* was made possible through a collaboration between the E-Governance Institute at Rutgers University-Newark and the Department of Public Policy and Public Affairs, John W. McCormack Graduate School of Policy and Global Studies at the University of Massachusetts Boston.

We would also like to express our deepest thanks to the evaluators for their contributions to this project. Their participation truly makes the research project successful. On the following page we list the numerous evaluators of websites throughout the world as acknowledgement of their efforts.

2015-16 Digital Governance Evaluators

Lazim Ahmedi
Otgonbayar Ajykyei
Mehmet Akif Demircioglu
Nour Alayan
Jessica Alcántara
Maria Almada
Ana Alpirez
Heba Al-Nasser
Nasser Alqahtani
Abdulrahman Alrefai
Wail Alshammari
Alejandro Álvarez Nobell
Carlo Angeles
Israel Aragón
Hugo Asencio
Ioanna Athinodorou
Cenay Babaoglu
Mojtaba Babaei Hezehjan
Haykaz Baghyan
Farouq Banihamad
Marcelo Batalha
Edita Bednarova
Miriam Begnum
Ieva Beinarovica

Mouli Bentman
Sofie Bertram
Stephen Birtwistle
Rhett Bowlin
Jane Canfield
Rafaela Charalambous
Kirsten Collins
Clelia Colombo
Vlad Costea
Francesco Cotera
Anabel Cruz
Mihály Csótó
Michael Dahan
Felix Deat
Ghislaine Delaine
Naghmeh Ebadi
Shaza Elmahdi
Francesca Fanucci
Susana Ferreira
Nikola Gjorgievski
Shangwei Hu
Dmytro Iefremov
Alida Ismaili
Ana Ivanovska

Maggie Kamel
Daniel Jez
Jeroen Joukes
Dubravka Jurlina-
 Alibegovic
Andrea Kaindl
Minsung Kang
Haytham Karar
Kruno Karlovcec
Martin Karlsson
Jyldyz Kasymova
Narine Khachatryan
Nino Kilasonia
Meelis Kitsing
Christoph Kühn
Scarlett Lanzas
Sungyoon Lee
Nele Leosk
Cristina Lisii
Vidmantas Mačiukas
Elena Maggioni
Khalid Majrashi
Hanjin Mao
Ricardo Matheus

Alexandros Melidis
Maria Merisalo
Sean McKitrick
James McQuiston
Sylvia Mlynarska
Dolores Modic
Lucia Mokrá
Sean Mossey
Marcia Mundt
Andras Nemeslaki
Tetyana Nikitina
Theresa Niederle
Sirius Nierzydowski
Manuel Ochoa
Iris Palma
Sabin Pandelea
Cesar Perez
Velina Petrova
Mariam Pirtskhalaishvili

Edvardas Pocius
Carlo Vasquez
Daniel Polimac
Paula Vita
Yana Rachovska
Margaret Ramirez
Aleksandra Vonda
Belissa Rivas
Corina Wagner
Leonardo Rocha
Zeng Wei
Alexis Rojas
James Wrocklage
Guido Scorza
Chengxin Xu
Vladislav Shabanov
Shaoyan Yan
Razilya Shakirova
Miao Yan

Shugo Shinohara
Kostenok Yaroslava
Hasan Shuaib
Yin Yue
Igor Stojanovic
Batbold Zagdragchaa
Efthimios Tambouris
Alona Zhuzha
Filipp Tatarenko
Carlo Vasquez
Hogne Ulla
Paula Vita
Vira Usyk
Marie-Carin von
 Gumppenberg
Patricia Vasquez
Aleksandra Vonda

CHAPTER 1

Introduction

The Digital Governance in Municipalities Worldwide Survey research replicates surveys completed by the E-Governance Institute at Rutgers University-Newark in 2003, 2005, 2007, 2009, 2011-12, and 2013-14, and evaluates the practice of digital governance in large municipalities worldwide in 2015-16.

This continuing research evaluates the websites of municipalities in terms of digital governance and ranks them on a global scale. Simply stated, digital governance is comprised of both digital government (delivery of public services) and digital democracy (citizen participation in governance). Specifically, we analyzed privacy/security, usability, and content of websites, the type of online services currently being offered, and citizen engagement and participation through websites established by municipal governments (Holzer, Zheng, Manoharan, & Shark, 14). The methodology of the 2015-16 survey of municipal websites throughout the world mirrors our previous research in 2003, 2005, 2007, 2009, 2011-12, and 2013-14. This research focused on global cities based on their population size and the total number of individuals using the Internet in each nation. The top 100 most wired nations were identified using data from the International Telecommunication Union (ITU), an organization affiliated with the United Nations (UN). The largest city by population in each of these 100 nations was then selected for the study and used as a surrogate for all cities in each respective country.

To examine how local populations perceive their governments online, the study evaluated the official websites of each of these largest cities in their native languages. The websites were evaluated between August of 2015 and February of 2016. Of the 100 cities selected, all but three were found to have official municipal websites. Two cities, Damascus and Beirut, appeared to have official websites that were normally in operation but which were under construction or maintenance during the period of our evaluation. The website of a third city, Algiers, could not be located. The absence of three websites from the 100 cities marks a slight dip in a trend of website availability that has seen a steady increase. For the 2005 survey, 81 of the 100 cities had official websites, which increased to 86 for the 2007 survey, 87 for the 2009 survey, 92 for the 2011-12 survey, and 100 for the 2013-14 survey. It is possible that the problems with website availability in three Middle Eastern cities are the result of political instability, particularly in the case of Syria where there is ongoing civil war.

Our instrument for evaluating municipal websites consisted of five components: 1. Privacy and Security; 2. Usability; 3. Content; 4. Services; and 5. Citizen and Social Engagement. For each of these five components, our research applied 18 to 26 measures, and each measure was coded on a scale of four points (0, 1, 2, 3) or a dichotomy of two points (0, 3 or 0, 1). Additionally, in developing an overall score for each municipality, we have equally weighted each of the five categories to avoid skewing the research in favor of a particular category (regardless of the number of questions in each category). This reflects the same methods utilized in the previous studies. To ensure reliability, each municipal website was assessed in the native language by two evaluators, and in cases where significant variation (+ or – 10%) existed on the adjusted score between evaluators, websites were analyzed by a third evaluator.

Based on the 2015-16 evaluation, Seoul, Helsinki, Madrid, Hong Kong, and Prague have the highest evaluation scores. There were noticeable changes in the top ten cities compared to the 2013-14 study: Singapore, Toronto, Shanghai and Dubai are no longer in the top ten; joining the top ten since 2013-14 are Helsinki, Madrid, Tallinn and Vilnius. Seoul remained the highest-ranked city, and the gap between first and second cities has decreased since 2013-14, from 19.65 to 10.08. In some cases, the scores may have slightly declined from the previous study. Table 1-2 lists the top 20 municipalities in digital governance from 2011-12 through 2015-16, and Table 1-2 lists the 20 municipalities from the 2015-16 study, along with their scores in individual categories. Tables 1-3 to 1-7 show the top-ranked municipalities for 2015-16 in each of the five categories.

The following chapters represent the overall findings of the research:

Chapter 2 outlines the methodology utilized in determining the websites evaluated, as well as the instrument used in the evaluations. Our survey instrument uses 104 measures and we follow a rigorous approach for conducting the evaluations.

Chapter 3 presents the overall findings for the 2015-16 evaluation. The overall results are also broken down into results by continents, and by OECD and non-OECD member countries.

Chapter 4 provides a longitudinal assessment of the 2013-14 and 2015-16 evaluations, with comparisons among continents, e-governance categories and OECD and non-OECD member countries.

Chapter 5 focuses on the results of Privacy and Security with regard to municipal websites.

Chapter 6 looks at the Usability of municipal websites throughout the world.

Chapter 7 presents the findings for Content.

Chapter 8 addresses Services.

Chapter 9 concludes the focus of specific e-governance categories by presenting the findings of Citizen and Social Engagement online.

Chapter 10 takes a closer look at best practices.

Chapter 11 concludes this study, providing recommendations and discussion of significant findings.

Table 1-1. *Top Cities in Digital Governance 2011-12~2015-16*

	2011-12		2013-14		2015-16	
Rank	City	Score	City	Score	City	Score
1	Seoul	82.23	Seoul	85.8	Seoul	79.92
2	Toronto	64.31	New York	66.15	Helsinki	69.84
3	Madrid	63.63	Hong Kong	60.32	Madrid	69.24
4	Prague	61.72	Singapore	59.82	Hong Kong	67.56
5	Hong Kong	60.81	Yerevan	59.61	Prague	66.48
6	New York	60.49	Bratislava	58.31	Tallinn	62.10
7	Stockholm	60.26	Toronto	58.05	New York	62.02
8	Bratislava	56.74	Shanghai	56.02	Bratislava	60.34
9	London	56.19	Dubai	55.89	Yerevan	59.61
10	Shanghai	55.49	Prague	54.88	Vilnius	59.12
11	Vilnius	55.35	Vilnius	53.82	Buenos Aires	57.88
12	Vienna	54.79	Vienna	53.4	Tokyo	57.04
13	Helsinki	54.22	Oslo	52.52	Singapore	56.03
14	Auckland	53.19	Stockholm	52.25	Moscow	54.73
15	Dubai	53.18	London	51.9	Oslo	54.37
16	Singapore	52.21	Helsinki	51.27	Amsterdam	54.36
17	Moscow	51.77	Macao	48.69	Auckland	54.27
18	Copenhagen	50.06	Mexico City	47.01	London	52.54
19	Yerevan	49.97	Kuala Lumpur	46.16	Lisbon	51.68
20	Paris	48.65	Zurich	45.36	Sydney	50.08

Table 1-2. *Top 20 Cities in Digital Governance (2015-16)*

Rank	City	Overall	Privacy	Usability	Content	Services	Citizen and Social Engagement
1	Seoul	79.92	13.33	15.94	17.30	16.89	16.46
2	Helsinki	69.84	14.44	17.50	13.17	11.80	12.92
3	Madrid	69.24	12.22	16.56	15.56	13.44	11.46
4	Hong Kong	67.56	12.59	17.81	13.65	14.75	8.75
5	Prague	66.48	14.44	15.31	15.08	11.64	10.00
6	Tallinn	62.10	8.52	17.50	14.13	15.08	6.88
7	New York	62.02	12.59	14.06	15.71	13.61	6.04
8	Bratislava	60.34	11.85	17.19	13.97	7.54	9.79
9	Yerevan	59.61	3.70	17.81	14.92	12.13	11.04
10	Vilnius	59.12	14.44	15.63	12.22	10.16	6.67
11	Buenos Aires	57.88	11.85	16.25	10.00	10.82	8.96
12	Tokyo	57.04	8.89	18.13	12.54	13.11	4.38
13	Singapore	56.03	9.63	14.38	10.16	13.11	8.75
14	Moscow	54.73	2.59	16.88	13.97	12.13	9.17
15	Oslo	54.37	14.07	10.94	14.44	10.33	4.58
16	Amsterdam	54.36	10.37	14.38	12.86	11.97	4.79
17	Auckland	54.27	8.89	14.06	12.22	11.80	7.29
18	London	52.54	12.22	15.00	10.00	11.15	4.17
19	Lisbon	51.68	9.26	12.50	11.90	8.85	9.17
20	Sydney	50.08	8.15	15.94	10.16	10.00	5.83

Table 1-3. *Top 10 Cities in Privacy and Security (2015-16)*

Rank	City	Country	Privacy
1	Manama	Philippines	16.30
2	Prague	Czech Republic	14.44
3	Helsinki	Finland	14.44
3	Vilnius	Lithuania	14.44
5	Oslo	Norway	14.07
6	Seoul	Korea (Rep.)	13.33
7	Berlin	Germany	12.96
8	New York	United States	12.59
9	Hong Kong	China	12.59
10	Vienna	Austria	12.22
10	Madrid	Spain	12.22
10	London	United Kingdom	12.22

Table 1-4. *Top 10 Cities in Usability (2015-16)*

Rank	City	Country	Usability
1	Tokyo	Japan	18.13
2	Hong Kong	China	17.81
2	Yerevan	Armenia	17.81
4	Helsinki	Finland	17.50
4	Tallinn	Estonia	17.50
6	Bratislava	Slovakia	17.19
7	Moscow	Russian Federation	16.88
8	Madrid	Spain	16.56
9	Buenos Aires	Argentina	16.25
10	Seoul	Korea (Rep.)	15.94
10	Dubai	United Arab Emirates	15.94
10	Sydney	Australia	15.94

Table 1-5. *Top 10 Cities in Content (2015-16)*

Rank	City	Country	Content
1	Seoul	Korea (Rep.)	17.30
2	New York	United States	15.71
3	Madrid	Spain	15.56
4	Prague	Czech Republic	15.08
5	Yerevan	Armenia	14.92
6	Oslo	Norway	14.44
7	Tallinn	Estonia	14.13
8	Bratislava	Slovakia	13.97
8	Moscow	Russian Federation	13.97
8	Bogota	Colombia	13.97

Table 1-6. *Top 10 Cities in Service Delivery (2015-16)*

Rank	City	Country	Services
1	Seoul	Korea (Rep.)	16.89
2	Tallinn	Estonia	15.08
3	Hong Kong	China	14.75
4	Jerusalem	Israel	13.61
5	New York	United States	13.61
6	Madrid	Spain	13.44
7	Tokyo	Japan	13.11
7	Singapore	Singapore	13.11
9	Mexico City	Mexico	12.95
10	Bogota	Colombia	12.46

Table 1-7. *Top 10 Cities in Citizen and Social Engagement (2015-16)*

Rank	City	Country	CS Engagement
1	Seoul	Korea (Rep.)	16.46
2	Helsinki	Finland	12.92
3	Madrid	Spain	11.46
4	Yerevan	Armenia	11.04
5	Prague	Czech Republic	10.00
6	Bratislava	Slovakia	9.79
7	Moscow	Russian Federation	9.17
7	Lisbon	Portugal	9.17
9	Buenos Aires	Argentina	8.96
10	Hong Kong	China	8.75
10	Singapore	Singapore	8.75
10	Shanghai	China	8.75

The average score for digital governance in municipalities throughout the world in 2015-16 is 36.57, which represents an overall increase in score from 33.37 in 2013-14, 33.76 in 2011-2012, 35.93 in 2009, 33.37 in 2007, 33.11 in 2005, and 28.49 in 2003. The average score for municipalities in OECD countries is 48.51, while the average score in non-OECD countries is 30.42, both of which show increases from 2013-14. This study hopes to continue to showcase this progress. Therefore, it is important to evaluate digital governance in large municipalities throughout the world periodically. The next Worldwide Survey is planned for 2017-18, and will further provide insights into the direction and performance countries are taking in regard to e-governance throughout regions of the world.

CHAPTER 2

Methodology

The methodological steps taken by the 2015-16 survey of worldwide municipal websites mirror the previous research done in 2013-14, 2011-12, 2009, 2007, 2005, and 2003. The research focuses on cities throughout the world based on population size and the total number of Internet users in each nation. The identification of cities based on these factors proceeded through the utilization of statistics published by the International Telecommunication Union (ITU), an organization affiliated with the United Nations (UN). To determine the 100 most wired nations worldwide, information on the total number of online users was compiled from the ITU-UN. In each country, the largest city by population was then selected as a surrogate for all cities in that country.

The rationale for selecting the largest city by population among the most wired nations stems from the e-governance literature, which suggests that at the local level there is a positive relationship between population and e-governance capacity (Manoharan, 2013; Moon, 2002; Moon & deLeon, 2001; Musso, et. al., 2000). Cities were, further, evaluated in their native language to improve accuracy in accessing their e-governance capacity; as many English language websites worldwide are intended for use by tourists and other non-citizens, evaluations in the native language facilitate a view of websites as they are intended for use by citizens of each country. Of the 100 cities selected, 97 were found to have official city websites, and these were evaluated from September 2015 to May 2016. For the 2013-14 survey, all 100 cities had official websites, increasing from 92 in the 2011-12 survey and 87 in the 2009 survey. Thus, the adoption of e-governance websites among municipalities across the world has slightly decreased since the release of the 2013-14 survey. Table 2-1 (see next page) is a list of the 100 cities selected and the city websites are provided in Appendix A.

Table 2-1. *100 Cities Selected by Continent (2015-16)*

Africa (7)	
Addis Ababa (Ethiopia)	Johannesburg (South Africa)
Algiers (Algeria)	Port Louis (Mauritius)
Cairo (Egypt)	Tunis (Tunisia)
Casablanca (Morocco)	
Asia (36)	
Almaty (Kazakhstan)	Karachi (Pakistan)
Amman (Jordan)	Kathmandu (Nepal)
Baku (Azerbaijan)	Kuala Lumpur (Malaysia)
Bangkok (Thailand)	Manama (Bahrain)
Beirut (Lebanon)	Manila (Philippines)
Bishkek (Kyrgyzstan)	Muscat (Oman)
Colombo (Sri Lanka)	Riyadh (Saudi Arabia)
Damascus (Syria)	Sana'a (Yemen)
Delhi (India)	Seoul (Republic of Korea)
Dhaka (Bangladesh)	Shanghai (China)
Doha (Qatar)	Singapore (Singapore)
Dubai (United Arab Emirates)	Taipei (Taiwan)
Gaza (Palestine)	Tashkent (Uzbekistan)
Ho Chi Minh City (Vietnam)	Tbilisi (Georgia)
Hong Kong (Hong Kong, China)	Tehran (Iran)
Istanbul (Turkey)	Tokyo (Japan)
Jakarta (Indonesia)	Ulaanbaatar (Mongolia)
Jerusalem (Israel)	Yerevan (Armenia)
Europe (37)	
Amsterdam (Netherlands)	Moscow (Russian)
Athens (Greece)	Nicosia (Cyprus)
Belgrade (Serbia and Montenegro)	Oslo (Norway)
Berlin (Germany)	Paris (France)
Bratislava (Slovak Republic)	Prague (Czech Republic)
Brussels (Belgium)	Riga (Latvia)
Bucharest (Romania)	Rome (Italy)

Europe (37) *continued*	
Budapest (Hungary)	Sarajevo (Bosnia and Herzegovina)
Chisinau (Moldova)	Skopje (Macedonia)
Copenhagen (Denmark)	Sofia (Bulgaria)
Dublin (Ireland)	Stockholm (Sweden)
Helsinki (Finland)	Tallinn (Estonia)
Kiev (Ukraine)	Tirana (Albania)
Lisbon (Portugal)	Vienna (Austria)
Ljubljana (Slovenia)	Vilnius (Lithuania)
London (United Kingdom)	Warsaw (Poland)
Luxembourg City (Luxembourg)	Zagreb (Croatia)
Madrid (Spain)	Zurich (Switzerland)
Minsk (Belarus)	
North and Central America (9)	
Guatemala City (Guatemala)	San Juan (Puerto Rico)
Mexico City (Mexico)	San Salvador (El Salvador)
New York (United States)	Santo Domingo (Dominican Republic)
Panama City (Panama)	Toronto (Canada)
San Jose (Costa Rica)	
South America (9)	
Bogotá (Colombia)	Montevideo (Uruguay)
Buenos Aires (Argentina)	San Fernando (Trinidad and Tobago)
Caracas (Venezuela)	Santiago (Chile)
Guayaquil (Ecuador)	Sao Paulo (Brazil)
Lima (Peru)	
Oceania (2)	
Auckland (New Zealand)	Sydney (Australia)

Website Survey

The focus of the evaluation is the main city homepage of each of the countries evaluated. This is defined as the official website where information about city administration and online services are provided by the municipality. Worldwide, municipalities are constantly improving their official websites as they are the primary interface with citizens in the e-government paradigm (Holzer, Manoharan, & Van Ryzin, 2010). Our survey is intended to identify the best practices associated with developing content so as to increase e-governance capacity. The emphasis of cities, then, should be on the use of technologies to effectively provide and communicate government services.

Specifically, a municipal website should include information about available city services, along with such information related to the city council, mayor and executive branch, as well as other departments and services. In cases where this information was contained on separate homepages, evaluators examined whether these sites were linked to the menu on the main city homepage. If the website was not linked, it was excluded from the evaluation as it was not easily accessible by users.

E-Governance Survey Instrument

The Rutgers E-Governance Survey Instrument is the most comprehensive index in practice for e-governance research today, with 104 measures and five distinct categorical areas of e-governance research. These five components are: 1. Privacy and Security 2. Usability 3. Content 4. Services and 5. Citizen and Social Engagement. Table 2-2 summarizes the survey instrument, and Appendix B presents an overview of the criteria.

The following section highlights the specific design of our survey instrument, which consists of 104 measures, of which 43 are dichotomous. For the five e-governance components, our research applies 18 to 26 measures for each category; for the non-dichotomous questions, each measure was coded on a four-point scale (0, 1, 2, 3; see Table 2-3). In addition, to avoid skewing the research and data in favor of a particular category, we weight each of the five categories equally in the final score total. This occurs regardless of the number of questions in each category, and develops an overall weighted score in each category, which gives equal category weight. The dichotomous measures in the "service" and "citizen and social engagement" categories correspond with values on a four-point scale of "0" or "3"; dichotomous measures in "privacy" or "usability" correspond to ratings of "0" or "1" on the scale.

Table 2-2. *E-Governance Performance Measures*

E-Governance Category	Key Concepts	Raw Score	Weighted Score	Keywords
Privacy/ Security	19	27	20	Privacy policies, authentication, encryption, data management, cookies
Usability	20	32	20	User-friendly design, branding, length of homepage, targeted audience links or channels, and site search capabilities
Content	26	63	20	Access to current accurate information, public documents, reports, publications, and multimedia materials
Services	21	61	20	Transactional services—purchase or register, interaction between citizens, businesses and government
Citizen and Social Engagement	18	48	20	Online civic engagement/ policy deliberation, social media applications, citizen- based performance measurement
Total	**104**	**231**	**100**	

Table 2-3. *E-Governance Scale*

Scale	Description
0	Information about a given topic does not exist on the website
1	Information about a given topic exists on the website (including links to other information and e-mail addresses)
2	Downloadable items are available on the website (forms, audio, video, and other one-way transactions, popup boxes)
3	Services, transactions, or interactions can take place completely online (credit card transactions, applications for permits, searchable databases, use of cookies, digital signatures, restricted access)

A higher value was placed on some dichotomous measures, due to the relative value of the different e-government services being evaluated. For example, evaluators using our instrument in the "service" category were given the option of scoring websites as either a "0" or "3" when assessing whether a site allowed users to access their private information online (e.g., educational records, medical records, point total of driving violations, lost property). "No access" equated to a rating of "0". The justification behind this scoring followed the logic that allowing residents or employees to access private information online was a higher-order task that required more technical competence and was clearly an online service, or "3," as defined in Table 2-3. Therefore, having that service garnered a higher rating based on the technical sophistication necessary to implement it.

When assessing a site as to whether or not it had a privacy statement or policy, evaluators were given the choice of scoring the site as "0" or "1". The presence or absence of a privacy policy was clearly a content issue that emphasized placing information online and corresponded with a value of "1" on the scale outlined in Table 2-3. Unlike services, it often did not require further technical prowess. However, when evaluating the presence of certain technically sophisticated privacy measures, i.e. checking for viruses or requiring users to log in to access private information, evaluators were given the option of scoring websites as either a "0" or "3." The differential values assigned to dichotomous categories were useful in comparing the components of municipal websites with one another.

To ensure reliability, each municipal website was assessed by two evaluators, and in cases where significant variation (+ or − 10%) existed on the weighted score between evaluators, websites were analyzed a third time to determine where significant differences were occurring. Furthermore, an example for each measure indicated how to score the variable to increase accuracy. Evaluators were given comprehensive written instructions for assessing websites.

E-Governance Categories

This section details the five e-governance categories of security/privacy, usability, content, services and citizen and social engagement, and discusses the specific measures within each category that are used to evaluate websites. Security and privacy relates, specifically, to the privacy policies and issues related to authentication addressed by the website. Usability relates to the use of traditional web pages, forms, and search tools by the website to allow ease of navigation by the user to services. The content category relates to overall access to contact information, access to public documents, disability access, as well as access to multimedia and time sensitive information. The services section examines interactive services, services that allow users to purchase or pay for services, and the ability of users to apply or register for municipal events or services online. Lastly, the measures for citizen and social engagement examine how local governments are engaging citizens and providing mechanisms for citizens to participate in government decision-making online via surveys, social media, forums, and other e-participation mediums.

Privacy/Security

The presence of privacy policies has the potential to improve public perception and trust of government, and enable greater citizen engagement with government (Fudge and Manoharan, 2013). In this category, we analyzed the level of privacy and security present in municipal websites by focusing on two key issues: privacy policies and user authentication. In analyzing privacy policies, evaluators first determined if the privacy policy indeed existed and was available on every page that required data. It was important that the privacy policy be accessible on each page so that users could easily access it while navigating the website.

Next, evaluators turned to the specific details within the privacy policy. Particular interest was paid to determining if the policy identified which agency/ agencies were collecting information, and whether and what data was being collected from usage of the website. Evaluators also examined whether the website explained how this data was going to be used and the purpose of the data collected on the website. Also of importance was if the use or sale of such data to outside third party organizations was addressed in the policy. Evaluators then determined if the privacy policy addressed whether third party agencies or organizations were governed by the same privacy policies as the municipal website. For example, evaluators searched for evidence that the same measures applied to all organizations with access to such data. They also examined whether users of the website were given an option to decline disclosure of personal information to third parties, which included other municipal agencies, state and local government offices, or private sector businesses. Additionally, they analyzed policy statements in order to ascertain if individuals could petition for access to their personal data in order to contest inaccurate or incomplete information.

Evaluators also addressed managerial measures that limited access to data and addressed protection of user data. This was used to assess whether data was used for unauthorized purposes and what authority monitored this. This examination also entailed the use of encryption in data transmission, and whether or not there was a means used to store data on secure servers.

In line with the growing trend in delivering transparent information, municipalities often offer citizens access to public, and sometimes private, information online. This can proceed via a secure server or via other forms of requests for such data. We are also particularly concerned with the impact of the digital divide if public records are available only through the Internet or if municipalities insist on charging a fee for access to public records. We believe such limited access will limit the ability of all citizens in accessing such services. Our analysis, then, specifically addresses whether certain key information such as property tax, private information, court documents, etc. were made available to website users through multiple venues so as to limit the digital divide.

Evaluators then assessed whether websites used digital signatures to authenticate users and whether public or private information was accessible through a restricted area that required a password and/or registration. Next, we wanted to look at whether websites monitored citizen activity, which we felt was a critical aspect of the analysis. We were concerned that public agencies might use websites to monitor citizens or create profiles based on information they access online for a number of purposes. The concern focused on analysis and transparency by the website in the use of such monitoring. The use of cookies and web beacons to authenticate and customize experiences is typical of many modern websites. This often creates a more user friendly experience that efficiently guides users through their browsing. However, that technology can also be used to monitor Internet habits and to profile a website visitor, which may limit usage and create security concerns on the part of the user. Therefore, evaluators examined municipal privacy policies to determine whether they addressed the use of these cookies or Web beacons.

Usability

The second component of our evaluation examined the usability of municipal websites. Simply stated, we wanted to know if websites were "user-friendly." Stated in another manner, did they facilitate and encourage use via their design. To measure this "user friendliness" we adapted best practices and measures from other public and private sector research (Giga, 2000), and examined three types of website features: traditional Web pages, forms, and search tools.

In our evaluation of traditional web pages written using hypertext markup language (HTML), we examined issues such as branding and structure (e.g., consistent color, font, graphics, and page length). For example, we evaluated whether all pages used consistent color, formatting and default colors (e.g., blue links and purple visited links), underlined text to indicate links, and whether or not visited links changed colors. We also checked whether the website clearly described system hardware and software requirements. Such branding and structure speaks to the overall usability of the website and its graphic appeal.

One particularly important concern in the examination was the use of online forms by government websites. These forms were typically provided to users with regard to a number of issues, ranging from reporting crimes to contacting the government. In measuring whether or not these forms facilitated ease of use, our examination, in particular, focused on whether field labels aligned appropriately with each field, whether fields were accessible by keystroke (e.g., tabs), whether the cursor automatically placed itself in the first field, whether required fields were explicitly noted, and whether the tab order of fields was logical. For example, after a user filled out the first name and pressed the tab key, did the cursor automatically go to the surname field? Or did the page skip to another field such as zip (postal) code, only to return to the surname later? We also looked to see whether form-specific pages provided additional information about how to fix user errors; for example, did the user have to reenter information or did the site flag incomplete or erroneous forms before accepting them? Likewise, did the site generate a confirmation page after a form was submitted, or did it return users to the homepage?

Our investigation also scrutinized each municipality's homepage to determine whether it was too long (two or more screen lengths) and/or whether it made available alternative versions of long documents, such as PDF or DOC files. Having multiple document types appeals directly to the preferences of the user, whereas having a condensed homepage succinctly delivers relevant information to the user. We also looked for targeted audience links or channels for customizing a website for specific groups such as citizens, businesses or other public agencies. For example, did the website have such targeted audience links available on the homepage so as to draw attention to resources for these specific groups? Other considerations included the consistent use of navigation bars and links to the homepage on every page, the availability of a sitemap or hyperlinked outline of the entire website, and whether duplicated link names connected to the same content. We also assessed whether or not the website was customizable based on user preferences.

Finally, the usability analysis addressed search tools on municipal websites to determine whether help searching the site was available or if whether the search scope could be limited to specific site areas. For instance, were users able to search only in "public works" or "the mayor's office," or did the search tool always search the entire site? We also looked for advanced search features like exact phrase searching, the ability to match any or all words, and Boolean searching capabilities (e.g., the ability to use AND/OR/NOT operators), as well as a site's ability to sort search results by relevance or other criteria. The ability to sort such information in this manner leads to ease of use and alleviates frustrations in searching for specific information through the ability to more succinctly search for information on the website.

Content

The third component of our evaluation pertains to content. Content is extremely important and presents a dynamic concern that is critical in website development. For example, no matter how technologically advanced the website is, if the content is not current, if it is difficult to navigate, or if the information provided is incorrect, then it is not fulfilling its purpose. This shows a reluctance to embrace the key tenets of service delivery tied to e-governance. Hence, when examining website content, we examined five key areas: access to contact information (specifically, information about each agency represented on the website), public documents, access for those with disabilities, multimedia materials, and time sensitive information.

Exploring these concerns, evaluators looked for critical components that showed whether the content of the website was current. We looked not only for a schedule of agency offices hours and availability, but also for online access to public documents, as well as a municipal code or charter and/or agency mission statements and the minutes of public meetings. Access to information of this sort was of critical concern as it demonstrated both up-to-date information and information which was readily available for users. We determined whether all users could access budget information and publications, whether the sites offered content in more than one language, and whether they provided access to disabled users through either "bobby compliance" (disability access for the blind, http://www.cast.org/bobby) or disability access for deaf users via a TDD phone service. To gauge the use of multimedia, we examined each site for the availability of audio or video files of public events, speeches, or meetings. Time sensitive information examined included the use of a municipal website for emergency management and/or as an alert mechanism (e.g., a terrorism or severe weather alert). We also checked for time sensitive information such as job vacancies or a calendar of community events.

Services

An important aspect of e-governance is the provision of public services online. With regard to service, evaluators attempted to determine to what extent municipalities delivered services to their citizens. We subsequently divided municipal services into two different service types: those that allow citizens to interact with the municipality—which can be as basic as forms for requesting information or filing complaints—and those that allow users to register online for municipal events or services.

Regarding delivery of services that allow citizens to interact with their municipality, we examined whether or not the website provided advanced interactive services through which users can report crimes or violations, customize municipal homepages based on their needs (e.g., portal customization), and access private information like court, educational, or medical records online. The interactivity and method through which citizens could access such services was of critical importance. Evaluators determined if there was an electronic medium to utilize services, or if such service proceeded through forms that needed to be submitted in person.

In terms of enabling citizens to register online for municipal services, many municipalities allow online applications for a range of services as diverse as building permits and dog licenses. Some local governments are also using the Internet for procurement, allowing potential contractors to access requests for proposals or even bid online for municipal contracts. Others are chronicling the procurement process by listing the total number of bidders for a contract online, and in some cases listing contact information for bidders. These elements were all of critical importance to us in our evaluation as they showcased multiple services targeted toward different audiences.

One benefit of e-governance service delivery is transactional services such as online payment of public utility bills and parking tickets that allow citizens to directly pay bills, fees, and fines on the government website. Not only do cities and municipalities worldwide allow online users to file or pay local taxes or pay fines, in some cases around the world cities are even allowing users to register or purchase tickets online for events in city halls or arenas. Because many municipalities have developed such capacities to accept payments for municipal services and taxes on their websites, we examined whether all municipal websites studied had developed this capacity.

Citizen and Social Engagement

The fifth component of our instrument pertains to online citizen participation in government. This is a fairly recent area of focus of e-governance study, and the number of channels through which the government can communicate with governments and officials has increased, along with the proliferation of social media. As noted in the previous surveys, the Internet has proven to be a convenient mechanism through which citizens can interact with their government. Further, the interactions between the government and citizens can proceed through a number of formal channels linked to the website (chat, discussion forums, polls, online newsletter, or e-mail listserv, etc.), and through social media (Facebook Twitter, YouTube, etc). The Internet is a convenient mechanism through which citizen-users can engage their government, and therefore this became a concern for us in our evaluation. Hence, we continued to strengthen our survey instrument in this area in order to identify several ways in which public agencies at the local level were involving citizens in decision making processes and gauging citizen inputs.

Evaluation proceeded particularly through an identification of municipal use of the Internet to foster civic engagement and citizen participation in government. For example, we evaluated whether municipal websites allow users to provide online comments or feedback to individual agencies or elected officials. Data was garnered through measuring citizen interactions that utilize a number of media. For example, some municipalities use their websites to measure performance and publish the results of performance measurement activities online. Still others use online bulletin boards or other chat capabilities to gather input on public issues. Such online bulletin boards offer citizens opportunities to post ideas, comments, or opinions without stipulation of specific discussion topics, although in some cases we found that agencies were attempting to structure online discussions around policy issues or specific agencies. We also examined if social media outlets were available for citizens to interact with governments. Once again, we found that the potential for online participation is still in its early stages of development: very few public agencies offer online opportunities for civic engagement.

Evaluators also looked at whether local governments offered current information about municipal governance online or through an online newsletter or e-mail listserv, and whether they used Internet-based polls about specific local issues to garner opinions. These mediums of communication encourage activity on the part of citizens and keep users up to date on issues. Likewise, we examined whether communities allowed users to participate in, and view the results of, citizen satisfaction surveys online.

CHAPTER 3

Overall Results

The following chapter presents results for all evaluated municipal websites during 2015-16. Table 3-1 provides the rankings for the 97 municipal websites and their overall scores. The scores reflect the combined scores of each municipality's evaluation in the five e-governance component categories. The highest possible score for any one city website is 100. Seoul received a score of 79.92, making it the highest-ranked city website for 2015-16. Seoul's website has consistently ranked #1 overall and was the highest-ranked in 2013-14, 2011-12, 2009, 2007, 2005, and 2003, with respective scores of 85.80, 82.23, 84.74, 87.74, 81.70, and 73.48. Helsinki was the second-highest ranked website, with a score of 69.84, a slightly more than 10 point difference with Seoul, moving up from its sixteenth position and score of 51.27 in 2013-14. Madrid was the third highest-ranked municipal website, with a score of 69.24, moving up significantly from its 29th place ranking and score of 40.62 in 2013-14. Hong Kong ranked fourth with a score of 67.56 in 2015-16, dropping one place from its third position in 2013-14, but improving its score from 60.32. Prague completed the top 5 with a score of 66.48 compared to its 2013-14 score of 54.88 and position then as 10th.

The results of the overall rankings are separated by continent in Tables 3-2 through 3-7. The top-ranked cities for each continent are Johannesburg (Africa), Seoul (Asia), Helsinki (Europe), New York (North America), Auckland (Oceania), and Buenos Aires (South America). Helsinki replaced Bratislava as the highest-ranked city for European municipalities, and Buenos Aires replaced Sao Paulo among South American municipalities.

Table 3-1. *Overall E-Governance Rankings (2015-16)*

Rank	City	Country	Score
1	Seoul	Korea (Rep.)	79.92
2	Helsinki	Finland	69.84
3	Madrid	Spain	69.24
4	Hong Kong	China	67.56
5	Prague	Czech Republic	66.48
6	Tallinn	Estonia	62.10
7	New York	United States	62.02
8	Bratislava	Slovakia	60.34
9	Yerevan	Armenia	59.61
10	Vilnius	Lithuania	59.12
11	Buenos Aires	Argentina	57.88
12	Tokyo	Japan	57.04
13	Singapore	Singapore	56.03
14	Moscow	Russian Federation	54.73
15	Oslo	Norway	54.37
16	Amsterdam	Netherlands	54.36
17	Auckland	New Zealand	54.27
18	London	United Kingdom	52.54
19	Lisbon	Portugal	51.68
20	Sydney	Australia	50.08
21	Berlin	Germany	50.06
22	Zurich	Switzerland	49.61
23	Jerusalem	Israel	49.23
24	Istanbul	Turkey	49.03
25	Bogota	Colombia	48.65
26	Copenhagen	Denmark	48.31
27	Toronto	Canada	47.93
28	Ljubljana	Slovenia	47.85
29	Mexico City	Mexico	46.75
30	Manama	Bahrain	46.03
31	Vienna	Austria	45.12
32	Johannesburg	South Africa	44.88
33	Dubai	United Arab Emirates	43.85
34	Zagreb	Croatia	43.04
35	Kuala Lumpur	Malaysia	43.03
36	Rome	Italy	42.83
37	Sarajevo	Bosnia and Herzegovina	42.09
38	Dublin	Ireland	41.65
39	Shanghai	China	41.63

Rank	City	Country	Score
40	Tbilisi	Georgia	41.49
41	Paris	France	41.43
42	Taipei	Taiwan, Province of China	40.45
43	Sao Paulo	Brazil	38.11
44	Athens	Greece	37.95
45	Kiev	Ukraine	37.84
46	Tehran	Iran	36.75
47	Riga	Latvia	36.62
48	Nicosia	Cyprus	36.39
49	Brussels	Belgium	36.19
50	Santo Domingo	Chile	35.49
51	San Juan	Puerto Rico	32.19
52	Delhi	India	31.85
53	Luxembourg City	Luxembourg	31.62
54	Muscat	Oman	31.03
55	Doha	Qatar	30.36
56	San Jose	Costa Rica	30.04
57	Sofia	Bulgaria	29.62
58	Amman	Jordan	29.31
59	Bucharest	Romania	28.95
60	Cairo	Egypt	28.52
61	Almaty	Kazakhstan	28.37
62	Minsk	Belarus	27.15
63	Warsaw	Poland	26.13
64	Belgrade	Serbia and Montenegro	25.93
65	Ulaanbaatar	Mongolia	25.90
66	Budapest	Hungary	25.17
67	San Salvador	El Salvador	25.03
68	Montevideo	Uruguay	24.96
69	Jakarta	Indonesia	24.62
70	Panama City	Panama	24.05
71	Colombo	Sri Lanka	23.10
71	Stockholm	Sweden	23.10
73	Guayaquil	Ecuador	22.28
74	Tashkent	Uzbekistan	21.97
75	Karachi	Pakistan	21.07
76	Bangkok	Thailand	20.83
77	Tunis	Tunisia	20.79
78	Kathmandu	Nepal	20.76

continued

Table 3-1. *Overall E-Governance Rankings (2015-16) continued*

Rank	City	Country	Score
79	Chisinau	Moldova	20.50
80	Casablanca	Morocco	20.44
81	Dhaka	Bangladesh	20.19
82	San Fernando	Trinidad & Tobago	19.86
83	Ho Chi Minh	Vietnam	19.75
84	Skopje	Macedonia	19.12
85	Caracas	Venezuela	18.79
86	Bishkek	Kyrgyzstan	18.62
87	Port Louis	Mauritius	18.57
88	Guatemala City	Guatemala	16.95
89	Sana'a	Yemen	16.57
90	Santiago	Chile	16.56
91	Riyadh	Saudi Arabia	16.36
92	Lima	Peru	16.27
93	Tirana	Albania	15.74
94	Manila	Philippines	14.09
95	Gaza	Palestine	13.08
96	Addis Ababa	Ethiopia	11.81
97	Baku	Azerbaijan	10.09

Table 3-2. *Results of Evaluation of African Cities (2015-16)*

Rank	City	Overall	Privacy	Usability	Content	Services	CS Engagement
1	Johannes-burg	44.88	9.26	14.06	10.63	7.38	3.54
2	Cairo	28.52	6.67	12.50	5.24	3.28	0.83
3	Tunis	20.79	1.11	12.81	3.65	1.97	1.25
4	Casablanca	20.44	0.00	12.50	4.29	3.44	0.21
5	Port Louis	18.57	0.00	9.38	3.97	3.77	1.46
6	Addis Ababa	11.81	0.00	8.44	2.06	1.31	0.00

Table 3-3. *Results of Evaluation of Asian Cities (2015-16)*

Rank	City	Overall	Privacy	Usability	Content	Services	CS Engagement
1	Seoul	79.92	13.33	15.94	17.30	16.89	16.46
2	Hong Kong	67.56	12.59	17.81	13.65	14.75	8.75
3	Yerevan	59.61	3.70	17.81	14.92	12.13	11.04
4	Tokyo	57.04	8.89	18.13	12.54	13.11	4.38
5	Singapore	56.03	9.63	14.38	10.16	13.11	8.75
6	Jerusalem	49.23	8.15	11.25	12.06	13.61	4.17
7	Manama	46.03	16.30	9.69	4.60	8.36	7.08
8	Dubai	43.85	10.74	15.94	6.67	9.67	0.83
9	Kuala Lumpur	43.03	8.89	11.88	10.32	8.20	3.75
10	Shanghai	41.63	2.22	14.69	7.78	8.20	8.75
11	Tbilisi	41.49	6.30	15.31	7.14	8.36	4.38
12	Taipei	40.45	7.04	14.06	7.78	8.03	3.54
13	Tehran	36.75	7.41	9.38	6.67	7.05	6.25
14	Delhi	31.85	2.59	11.25	7.94	8.20	1.88
15	Muscat	31.03	4.07	13.44	4.29	5.90	3.33
16	Doha	30.36	4.44	12.81	4.92	6.72	1.46
17	Amman	29.31	4.07	11.88	5.40	4.43	3.54
18	Almaty	28.37	0.00	13.75	4.44	7.05	3.13
19	Ulaanbaatar	25.90	2.22	10.00	9.52	3.11	1.04
20	Jakarta	24.62	0.00	11.25	7.94	3.77	1.67
21	Colombo	23.10	1.11	11.56	4.13	4.43	1.88
22	Tashkent	21.97	0.37	9.38	4.76	4.75	2.71
23	Karachi	21.07	1.11	10.63	4.76	3.11	1.46
24	Bangkok	20.83	3.70	10.94	3.81	1.97	0.42
25	Kathmandu	20.76	1.11	10.94	3.81	3.44	1.46
26	Dhaka	20.19	0.56	10.94	4.05	3.61	1.04
27	Ho Chi Minh	19.75	3.33	7.81	5.40	2.79	0.42
28	Bishkek	18.62	0.00	10.00	5.24	2.13	1.25
29	Sana'a	16.57	0.00	13.44	2.06	0.66	0.42
30	Riyadh	16.36	0.00	7.81	5.08	1.80	1.67
31	Manila	14.09	1.85	6.56	2.22	2.62	0.83
32	Gaza	13.08	0.00	7.50	2.38	2.79	0.42
33	Baku	10.09	0.00	7.50	2.38	0.00	0.21

Table 3-4. *Results of Evaluation of European Cities (2015-16)*

Rank	City	Overall	Privacy	Usability	Content	Services	CS Engagement
1	Helsinki	69.84	14.44	17.50	13.17	11.80	12.92
2	Madrid	69.24	12.22	16.56	15.56	13.44	11.46
3	Prague	66.48	14.44	15.31	15.08	11.64	10.00
4	Tallinn	62.10	8.52	17.50	14.13	15.08	6.88
5	Bratislava	60.34	11.85	17.19	13.97	7.54	9.79
6	Vilnius	59.12	14.44	15.63	12.22	10.16	6.67
7	Moscow	54.73	2.59	16.88	13.97	12.13	9.17
8	Oslo	54.37	14.07	10.94	14.44	10.33	4.58
9	Amsterdam	54.36	10.37	14.38	12.86	11.97	4.79
10	London	52.54	12.22	15.00	10.00	11.15	4.17
11	Lisbon	51.68	9.26	12.50	11.90	8.85	9.17
12	Berlin	50.06	12.96	12.81	9.84	8.20	6.25
13	Zurich	49.61	7.04	15.31	13.81	8.03	5.42
14	Stockholm	49.18	8.15	15.31	13.02	7.70	5.00
15	Istanbul	49.03	9.63	12.50	11.59	11.15	4.17
16	Copenhagen	48.31	7.41	13.44	11.27	10.98	5.21
17	Ljubljana	47.85	7.41	11.88	13.81	9.34	5.42
18	Vienna	45.12	12.22	10.94	12.70	4.26	5.00
19	Zagreb	43.04	9.63	12.81	8.57	8.69	3.33
20	Rome	42.83	11.85	10.00	10.95	8.36	1.67
21	Sarajevo	42.09	7.41	14.06	8.73	6.89	5.00
22	Dublin	41.65	7.78	12.50	7.30	8.03	6.04
23	Paris	41.43	7.41	9.06	9.68	8.20	7.08
24	Athens	37.95	7.04	13.13	6.51	8.36	2.92
25	Kiev	37.84	3.70	15.31	10.32	4.75	3.75
26	Riga	36.62	6.30	11.25	9.05	8.36	1.67
27	Nicosia	36.39	5.93	13.13	5.40	8.20	3.75
28	Brussels	36.19	4.07	15.31	7.46	7.05	2.29
29	Luxembourg City	31.62	0.00	15.31	7.30	4.43	4.58
30	Sofia	29.62	7.78	11.88	5.56	2.95	1.46
31	Bucharest	28.95	1.85	15.31	5.87	2.79	3.13
32	Minsk	27.15	3.70	10.63	4.29	3.11	5.42
33	Warsaw	26.13	8.15	10.31	4.29	2.13	1.25
34	Belgrade	25.93	0.00	12.50	7.46	4.10	1.88
35	Budapest	25.17	0.00	10.63	8.57	4.10	1.88
36	Chisinau	20.50	0.00	10.94	4.44	2.62	2.50
37	Skopje	19.12	1.85	8.13	4.76	2.30	2.08
38	Tirana	15.74	0.00	10.63	4.13	0.98	0.00

Table 3-5. *Results of Evaluation of North American Cities (2015-16)*

Rank	City	Overall	Privacy	Usability	Content	Services	CS Engagement
1	New York	62.02	12.59	14.06	15.71	13.61	6.04
2	Toronto	47.93	7.41	14.69	11.90	9.34	4.58
3	Mexico City	46.75	5.19	11.88	11.11	12.95	5.63
4	Santo Domingo	35.49	5.56	12.50	8.10	4.75	4.58
5	San Juan	32.19	11.85	9.69	4.13	5.90	0.63
6	San Jose	30.04	2.96	10.31	7.14	7.54	2.08
7	San Salvador	25.03	2.59	9.38	8.25	3.77	1.04
8	Panama City	24.05	4.07	9.06	6.51	2.95	1.46
9	Guatemala City	16.95	1.11	7.81	4.29	3.11	0.63

Table 3-6. *Results of Evaluation of Oceanic Cities (2015-16)*

Rank	City	Overall	Privacy	Usability	Content	Services	CS Engagement
1	Auckland	54.27	8.89	14.06	12.22	11.80	7.29
2	Sydney	50.08	8.15	15.94	10.16	10.00	5.83

Table 3-7. *Results of Evaluation of South American Cities (2015-16)*

Rank	City	Overall	Privacy	Usability	Content	Services	CS Engagement
1	Buenos Aires	57.88	11.85	16.25	10.00	10.82	8.96
2	Bogota	48.65	2.22	15.00	13.97	12.46	5.00
3	Sao Paulo	38.11	3.33	12.81	9.84	9.84	2.29
4	Montevideo	24.96	0.00	12.19	6.19	4.92	1.67
5	Guayaquil	22.28	2.22	13.13	3.97	2.13	0.83
6	San Fernando	19.86	0.00	10.00	5.08	3.11	1.67
7	Caracas	18.79	1.11	7.50	4.92	4.43	0.83
8	Santiago	16.56	0.00	8.44	7.30	0.82	0.00
9	Lima	16.27	0.37	6.88	6.51	1.48	1.04

The average scores for each continent are presented in Figure 3-1. Oceania was again the highest-ranked continent, with an average score of 52.17, and Europe, with a score of 43.16 remained in the second highest rank. North America and Asia followed with scores of 35.61 and 33.35 respectively. South America had an overall score of 29.26, and Africa had a score of 24.17. The overall average score for all municipalities worldwide was 36.57, an increase from 33.37 in 2013-14. Although North America is ranked fourth among the continents, it includes a wide range of performance with cities such as New York, Toronto, and Mexico City ranked among the top 30 cities overall, representing advanced e-government practices, while others were ranked significantly lower among the cities evaluated.

Table 3-8. *Average Score by Continent (2015-16)*

	Oceania	Europe	Asia	Average	North America	South America	Africa
Overall Averages	52.17	43.16	33.35	36.57	35.61	29.26	24.17

Fig 3-1. *Average Score by Continent (2015-16)*

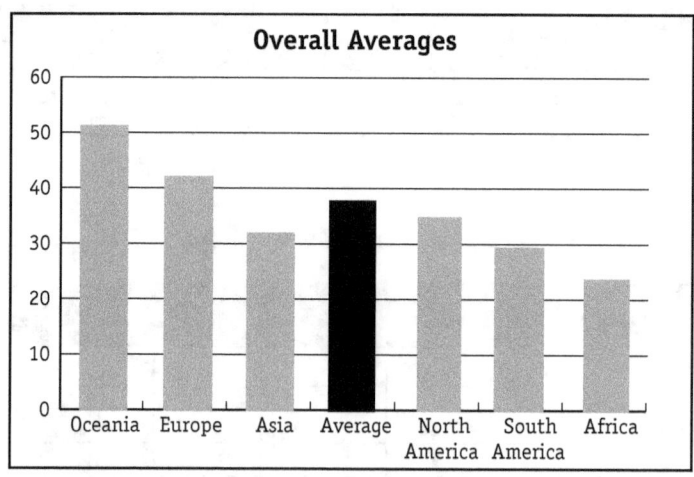

OECD Member Data

Seoul remained as the highest-ranked OECD municipality with a score of 79.92, and Hong Kong remained the highest-ranked non-OECD in 2015-16 with a score of 67.56. Tables 3-9 and 3-10 present the overall score for each municipality, grouped into OECD member countries and non-OECD member countries.

Table 3-9. *Results for OECD Member Countries (2015-16)*

Rank	City	Country	Score
1	Seoul	Korea (Rep.)	79.92
2	Helsinki	Finland	69.84
3	Madrid	Spain	69.24
4	Prague	Czech Republic	66.48
5	Tallinn	Estonia	62.10
6	New York	United States	62.02
7	Bratislava	Slovakia	60.34
8	Tokyo	Japan	57.04
9	Oslo	Norway	54.37
10	Amsterdam	Netherlands	54.36
11	Auckland	New Zealand	54.27
12	London	United Kingdom	52.54
13	Lisbon	Portugal	51.68
14	Sydney	Australia	50.08
15	Berlin	Germany	50.06
16	Zurich	Switzerland	49.61
17	Jerusalem	Israel	49.23
18	Istanbul	Turkey	49.03
19	Copenhagen	Denmark	48.31
20	Toronto	Canada	47.93
21	Ljubljana	Slovenia	47.85
22	Mexico City	Mexico	46.75
23	Vienna	Austria	45.12
24	Rome	Italy	42.83
25	Dublin	Ireland	41.65
26	Paris	France	41.43
27	Athens	Greece	37.95
28	Brussels	Belgium	36.19
29	Luxembourg City	Luxembourg	31.62
30	Warsaw	Poland	26.13
31	Budapest	Hungary	25.17
32	Stockholm	Sweden	23.10
33	Santiago	Chile	16.56

Table 3-10. *Results for OECD Non-Member Countries (2015-16)*

Rank	City	Country	Score
1	Hong Kong	China	67.56
2	Yerevan	Armenia	59.61
3	Vilnius	Lithuania	59.12
4	Buenos Aires	Argentina	57.88
5	Singapore	Singapore	56.028
6	Moscow	Russian Federation	54.734
7	Bogota	Colombia	48.65
8	Manama	Bahrain	46.03
9	Johannesburg	South Africa	44.875
10	Dubai	United Arab Emirates	43.85
11	Zagreb	Croatia	43.035
12	Kuala Lumpur	Malaysia	43.03
13	Sarajevo	Bosnia and Herzegovina	42.09
14	Shanghai	China	41.63
15	Tbilisi	Georgia	41.49
16	Taipei	Taiwan, Province of China	40.452
17	Sao Paulo	Brazil	38.11
18	Kiev	Ukraine	37.84
19	Tehran	Iran	36.748
20	Riga	Latvia	36.62
21	Nicosia	Cyprus	36.39
22	Santo Domingo	Dominican Republic	35.49
23	San Juan	Puerto Rico	32.19
24	Delhi	India	31.851
25	Muscat	Oman	31.03
26	Doha	Qatar	30.357
27	San Jose	Costa Rica	30.043
28	Sofia	Bulgaria	29.62
29	Amman	Jordan	29.31
30	Bucharest	Romania	28.95
31	Cairo	Egypt	28.517
32	Almaty	Kazakhstan	28.37
33	Minsk	Belarus	27.15
34	Belgrade	Serbia and Montenegro	25.93
35	Ulaanbaatar	Mongolia	25.902
36	San Salvador	El Salvador	25.034
37	Montevideo	Uruguay	24.96
38	Jakarta	Indonesia	24.624
39	Panama City	Panama	24.05

Rank	City	Country	Score
40	Colombo	Sri Lanka	23.102
41	Guayaquil	Ecuador	22.28
42	Tashkent	Uzbekistan	21.97
43	Karachi	Pakistan	21.071
44	Bangkok	Thailand	20.835
45	Tunis	Tunisia	20.792
46	Kathmandu	Nepal	20.759
47	Chisinau	Moldova	20.505
48	Casablanca	Morocco	20.437
49	Dhaka	Bangladesh	20.189
50	San Fernando	Trinidad & Tobago	19.86
51	Ho Chi Minh	Vietnam	19.746
52	Skopje	Macedonia	19.117
53	Caracas	Venezuela	18.791
54	Bishkek	Kyrgyzstan	18.619
55	Port Louis	Mauritius	18.57
56	Guatemala City	Guatemala	16.95
57	Sana'a	Yemen	16.57
58	Riyadh	Saudi Arabia	16.362
59	Lima	Peru	16.27
60	Tirana	Albania	15.736
61	Manila	Philippines	14.09
62	Gaza	Palestine	13.08
63	Addis Ababa	Ethiopia	11.812
64	Baku	Azerbaijan	10.09

The results above for OECD and Non-OECD countries are analyzed in the following as well through an analysis of their grouped averages. Figure 3-2 (see next page) highlights how the OECD member countries have a combined average of 48.51. This is well above the overall average for all municipalities (36.57), and higher than their previous score from 2013-14 (43.24). Non-OECD member countries have an overall average of 30.42, which represents a substantial increase in their score from 2013-14 (28.51).

Further, examination shows the differences between OECD and Non-OECD countries among the five e-governance categories.

Table 3-11 (see next page) presents the scores for OECD member countries, non-OECD member countries, and overall average scores for each of the e-governance categories. The results are the same as from the 2013-14 analysis. Specifically, in distinguishing between the scores, it can be seen that the average score for OECD member countries in each e-governance category is higher than the overall average score in each e-governance category. Further, for non-OECD member countries, the average scores in each category are lower than the overall averages for each category. The results of the evaluation are discussed in further detail in the following chapters.

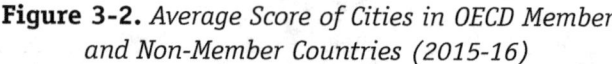

Figure 3-2. *Average Score of Cities in OECD Member and Non-Member Countries (2015-16)*

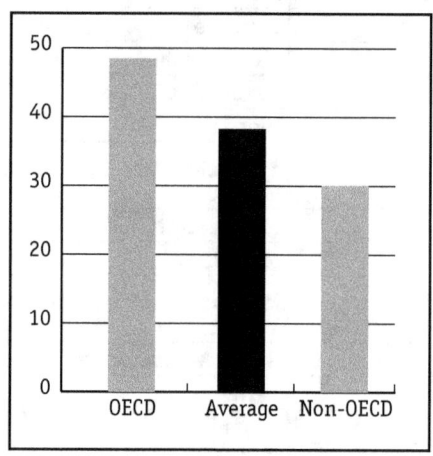

Table 3-11. *Average Score of E-Governance Categories in OECD Member and Non-Member Countries (2015-16)*

	Privacy/ Security	Usability	Content	Service	CS Engagement
OECD	8.82	13.63	11.5	9.52	5.83
Overall Average	5.55	12.38	8.22	6.82	3.87
Non-OECD	3.86	11.74	6.53	5.43	2.86

CHAPTER 4

Longitudinal Assessment

This chapter outlines the comparison between the findings from the 2013-14, 2011-12, 2009, 2007, 2005 and 2003 evaluations and the findings of the 2015-16 evaluation. The overall average score for all municipalities surveyed around the world was 36.57, an overall increase from 33.37 in 2013-14, 33.76 in 2011-2012, 35.93 in 2009, 33.37 in 2007, 33.11 in 2005, and 28.49 in 2003 (as shown in Figure 4-1).

Compared to 2013-14, there was an increase in all five average e-governance categories in 2015-16. Because of this, the overall average score in 2015-16 was higher than in 2013-14. Table 4-1 and Figure 4-2 (see page 35) highlight the differences and changes by continent.

Figure 4-1. *Average E-Governance Score 2003–2015-16*

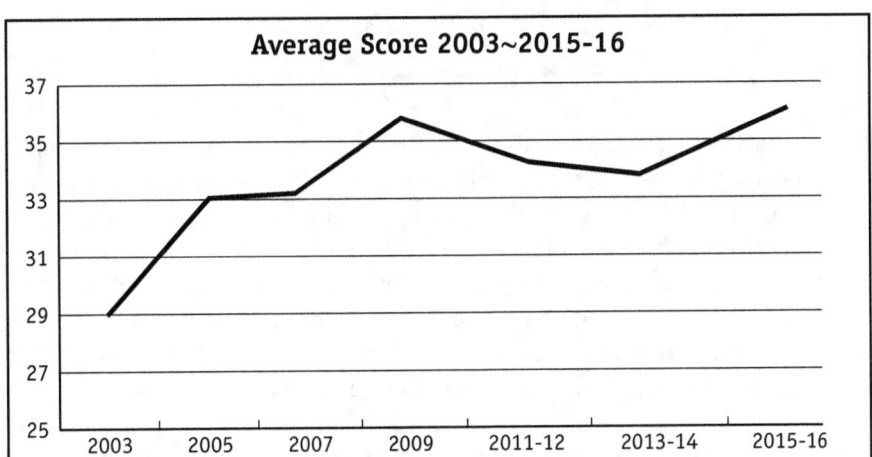

Table 4-1. *Average Score by Continent 2003–2015-16*

	Oceania	Europe	Asia	Average	North America	South America	Africa
2015-16 Overall Averages	52.17	43.16	33.35	**36.57**	35.61	29.26	24.17
2013-14 Overall Averages	41.08	36.2	33.1	**33.37**	31.96	31.37	21.18
2011-12 Overall Averages	41.85	39.95	31.85	**33.76**	30.99	28.44	21.06
2009 Overall Averages	48.59	39.54	37.13	**35.93**	32.65	31.23	24.06
2007 Overall Averages	47.37	37.55	33.26	**33.37**	33.77	28.2	16.87
2005 Overall Averages	49.94	37.17	33.05	**33.11**	30.21	20.45	24.87
2003 Overall Averages	46.01	30.23	30.38	**28.49**	27.42	20.25	17.66

Oceania was the highest ranked continent, with an average score of 52.17, which was much higher than its score of 41.08 in 2013-14. Europe, with a score of 43.16, remained in the second highest rank, and also increased its score of 36.20 in 2013-14. This was followed by Asia and North America, with scores of 33.35 and 35.61, respectively, modest increases from their scores of 33.10 and 31.96 in 2013-14. South America and Africa follow with scores of 29.26 and 24.17 respectively. While Africa increased its score from 21.17 in 2013-14, South America dropped slightly from its score of 31.37 in 2013-14.

Further, our survey results indicate that the number of cities with official websites is 97% in 2015-16. This shows that most cities have not lost or suspended their websites. The changes in scores from 2003 to 2015-16, represented by both OECD and non-OECD member countries, are shown in Table 4-2.

Figure 4-2. *Average Score by Continent for 2003–2015-16*

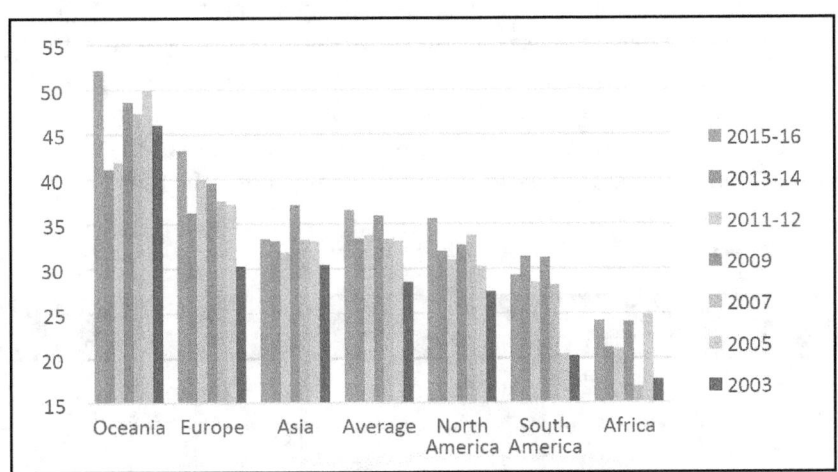

Table 4-2. *Average Scores by OECD Member and Non-Member Countries 2003–2015-16*

	OECD	Average	Non-OECD
2015-16 Overall Averages	48.51	**36.57**	30.42
2013-14 Overall Averages	43.24	**33.37**	28.51
2011-12 Overall Averages	45.45	**33.76**	27.52
2009 Overall Averages	46.69	**35.93**	30.83
2007 Overall Averages	45	**33.37**	27.46
2005 Overall Averages	44.35	**33.11**	26.5
2003 Overall Averages	36.34	**28.49**	24.36

Municipalities surveyed from OECD member countries increased their average score from 43.24 to 48.51. In addition, municipalities surveyed from non-OECD member countries increased their average score from 28.51 to 30.42. Among the five categories (Privacy/Security, Usability, Content, Services, and Citizen and Social Engagement), all improved slightly in 2015-16 as compared to 2013-14.

The category of Usability remained as the highest average score among the five categories, and Citizen and Social Engagement remained as the category with the lowest average score. These results show that cities have too often been hesitant to adopt citizen-centric participatory e-governance services, and have yet to recognize the importance of involving and supporting citizen participation online. Specific increases in the five e-governance categories are discussed in the following chapters. Table 4-3 and Figure 4-4 highlight these findings.

Table 4-3. *Average Score by E-Governance Categories 2003–2015-16*

	Privacy/ Security	Usability	Content	Service	CS Engagement
2015-16 Overall Averages	5.55	12.38	8.22	6.82	3.87
2013-14 Overall Averages	4.88	12.04	7.62	5.49	3.34
2011-12 Overall Averages	4.99	12.09	7.38	5.78	3.53
2009 Overall Averages	5.57	11.96	8.21	6.68	3.5
2007 Overall Averages	4.49	11.95	7.58	5.8	3.55
2005 Overall Averages	4.17	12.42	7.63	5.32	3.57
2003 Overall Averages	2.53	11.45	6.43	4.82	3.26

Figure 4-4. *Average Score by Categories 2003–2015-16*

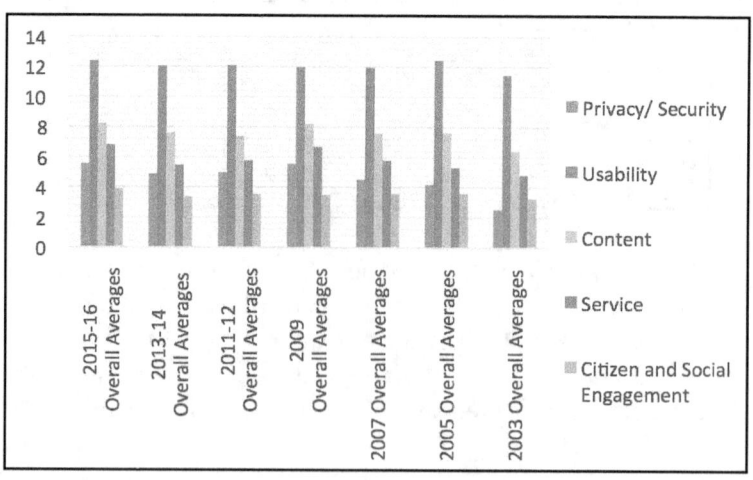

CHAPTER 5

Privacy and Security

Privacy and security results show that the top-ranked cities in 2015-16 are Manama, Prague, Helsinki, Vilnius, and Oslo. Manama improved its position markedly from 78th to 1st; this capped a staggering change in position from 2013-14 from a score of 0 to a score of 16.30 in 2015-16 out of a maximum score of 20. Prague, Helsinki, and Vilnius share the second place position with scores of 14.44. Prague was ranked 3rd in 2013-14, but has improved to the 2nd position in overall ranking, with a score of 14.44 in 2015-16. Helsinki also improved its score to 14.44 compared to the 2013-14 score of 13.70. Vilnius, dropped slightly, but remained in the 2nd position. Its score in 2015-16 is 14.44 compared to the previous score of 15.56 in 2013-14. In the fifth position was Oslo, which had the same score of 14.07 as in 2013-14. Table 5-1 summarizes the results for all municipalities evaluated in this category.

The average score in this category was 5.55, an increase from a score of 4.88 in 2013-14. There was also a decrease in the number of cities that earned 0 points in this category in 2015-16. Only eighteen cities earned scores of 0, compared to twenty-three cities so evaluated in 2013-14.

Table 5-1. *Results in Privacy and Security (2015-16)*

Rank	City	Country	Privacy
1	Manama	Bahrain	16.30
2	Prague	Czech Republic	14.44
3	Helsinki	Finland	14.44
3	Vilnius	Lithuania	14.44
5	Oslo	Norway	14.07
6	Seoul	Korea (Rep.)	13.33
7	Berlin	Germany	12.96
8	New York	United States	12.59
9	Hong Kong	China	12.59
10	Madrid	Spain	12.22
10	London	United Kingdom	12.22
10	Vienna	Austria	12.22
13	Bratislava	Slovakia	11.85

continued

Rank	City	Country	Privacy
13	Buenos Aires	Argentina	11.85
13	Rome	Italy	11.85
13	San Juan	Puerto Rico	11.85
17	Dubai	United Arab Emirates	10.74
18	Amsterdam	Netherlands	10.37
19	Singapore	Singapore	9.63
19	Istanbul	Turkey	9.63
19	Zagreb	Croatia	9.63
22	Lisbon	Portugal	9.26
22	Johannesburg	South Africa	9.26
24	Tokyo	Japan	8.89
24	Auckland	New Zealand	8.89
24	Kuala Lumpur	Malaysia	8.89
27	Tallinn	Estonia	8.52
28	Sydney	Australia	8.15
28	Warsaw	Poland	8.15
28	Stockholm	Sweden	8.15
31	Jerusalem	Israel	8.15
32	Dublin	Ireland	7.78
32	Sofia	Bulgaria	7.78
34	Copenhagen	Denmark	7.41
35	Toronto	Canada	7.41
35	Ljubljana	Slovenia	7.41
35	Sarajevo	Bosnia and Herzegovina	7.41
35	Paris	France	7.41
35	Tehran	Iran	7.41
40	Zurich	Switzerland	7.04
40	Taipei	Taiwan, Province of China	7.04
40	Athens	Greece	7.04
43	Cairo	Egypt	6.67
44	Tbilisi	Georgia	6.30
45	Riga	Latvia	6.30
46	Nicosia	Cyprus	5.93
47	Santo Domingo	Dominican Republic	5.56
48	Mexico City	Mexico	5.19
49	Doha	Qatar	4.44
50	Brussels	Belgium	4.07
50	Muscat	Oman	4.07
50	Amman	Jordan	4.07
50	Panama City	Panama	4.07
54	Yerevan	Armenia	3.70
55	Kiev	Ukraine	3.70

Rank	City	Country	Privacy
55	Minsk	Belarus	3.70
55	Bangkok	Thailand	3.70
58	Sao Paulo	Brazil	3.33
58	Ho Chi Minh	Vietnam	3.33
60	San Jose	Costa Rica	2.96
61	Moscow	Russian Federation	2.59
61	Delhi	India	2.59
61	San Salvador	El Salvador	2.59
64	Bogota	Colombia	2.22
64	Shanghai	China	2.22
64	Ulaanbaatar	Mongolia	2.22
64	Guayaquil	Ecuador	2.22
68	Bucharest	Romania	1.85
68	Skopje	Macedonia	1.85
68	Manila	Philippines	1.85
71	Colombo	Sri Lanka	1.11
71	Karachi	Pakistan	1.11
71	Tunis	Tunisia	1.11
71	Kathmandu	Nepal	1.11
71	Caracas	Venezuela	1.11
71	Guatemala City	Guatemala	1.11
77	Dhaka	Bangladesh	0.56
78	Tashkent	Uzbekistan	0.37
78	Lima	Peru	0.37
80	Luxembourg City	Luxembourg	0.00
80	Almaty	Kazakhstan	0.00
80	Belgrade	Serbia and Montenegro	0.00
80	Budapest	Hungary	0.00
80	Montevideo	Uruguay	0.00
80	Jakarta	Indonesia	0.00
80	Chisinau	Moldova	0.00
80	Casablanca	Morocco	0.00
80	San Fernando	Trinidad & Tobago	0.00
80	Bishkek	Kyrgyzstan	0.00
80	Port Louis	Mauritius	0.00
80	Sana'a	Yemen	0.00
80	Santiago	Chile	0.00
80	Riyadh	Saudi Arabia	0.00
80	Tirana	Albania	0.00
80	Gaza	Palestine	0.00
80	Addis Ababa	Ethiopia	0.00
80	Baku	Azerbaijan	0.00

Table 5-2 represents the average scores of nations in Privacy and Security by continent. Oceania remained as the continent with the highest average scores, with 8.52 points, followed by Europe, with 7.47 points. Africa was still the continent with the lowest average score, with 2.84 points. Asia and South America dropped slightly in score from their 2013-14 values, but all other continents increased in score.

As shown in Figure 5-2, cities in OECD countries scored an average of 8.82, while cities in non-member countries scored only 3.86 in this category. These results indicate that cities in economically advanced countries continue to have more emphasis on privacy and security policy than do cities in less developed countries. However, both member and non-member countries saw an increase in their overall average score. Figure 5-1 illustrates the data presented in Table 5-2.

Figure 5-1. *Average Score in Privacy and Security by Continent (2015-16)*

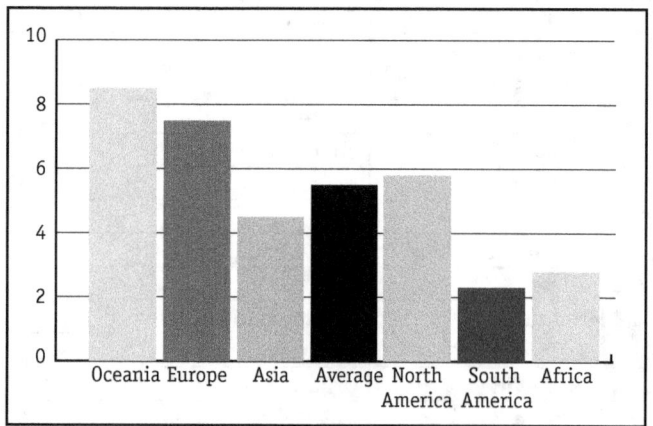

Table 5-2. *Average Score in Privacy/Security by Continent (2015-16)*

	Oceania	Europe	Asia	Average	North America	South America	Africa
Privacy Averages	8.52	7.47	4.42	5.55	5.93	2.35	2.84

Figure 5-2. *Average Score in Privacy and Security by OECD Member and Non-Member Countries (2015-16)*

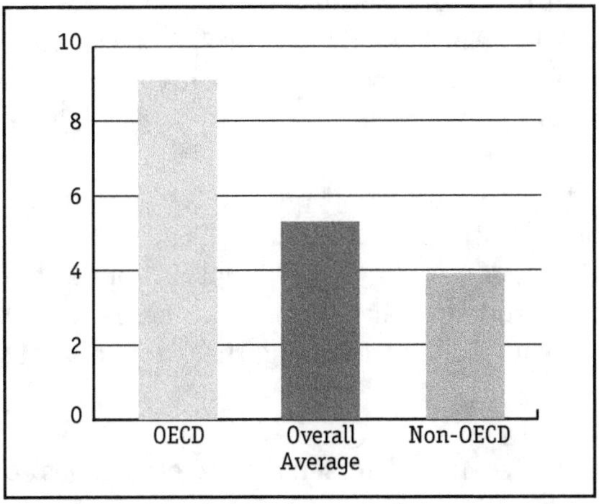

Table 5-3 lists the results of the evaluation of key aspects in the category of Privacy and Security by continent. All cities in Oceania had a privacy and security statement/policy, as did 82% of cities in Europe, 52% in Asia, 78% in North America, 22% in South America, and 33% in Africa. In all continents, except South America, there has been a rise in the percentage of posted policies since 2013-14. The overall average percentage for cities that have a privacy or security policy online is 61%, a rise of 11% from 50% in 2013-14.

Table 5-3. *Results for Privacy and Security by Continent (2015-16)*

	Oceania	Europe	Asia	Average	North America	South America	Africa
Privacy or Security Policy	100%	82%	52%	61%	78%	22%	33%
Use of Encryption	50%	26%	21%	27%	22%	11%	33%
Use of Cookies	100%	61%	24%	41%	33%	11%	17%
Digital Signature	0%	21%	6%	6%	0%	11%	0%

With regard to the use of encryption in the transmission of data, 27% of all cities globally have addressed this issue, a rise from 22% in 2013-14. Oceania once again leads with 50% of cities using encryption, followed by Africa with 33%, Europe with 26%, North America with 22%, Asia with 21%, and South America with 11%. Overall, 27% of cities explicitly noted the use of encryption in their privacy/security policies.

The overall percentage for cities that provide the option of digital signatures is 6%, a rise of only 1% from the 5% found in 2013-14. This is compared to 41% of all cities that address the use of "cookies" or "web beacons" to track users, a rise of 16% from 25% in 2013-14. No cities worldwide in the 2003 evaluation had a privacy policy addressing the use of digital signatures to authenticate users.

All cities evaluated in Oceania addressed the use of "cookies" or "web beacons." They were followed by 36% of cities in Europe, 33% in North America, 24% in Asia, 17% of in Africa, and 11% in South America. Save for cities in South America, all continents advanced in addressing the use of "cookies" or "web beacons". The overall average percentage for cities that addressed the use of "cookies" is 41%, a 16% increase from 25% in 2013-14.

Table 5-4 lists the results of the evaluation of key aspects in the category of Privacy and Security for OECD and non-OECD member countries. Overall, these results are consistent with those of previous years in that OECD countries continue to pay far greater attention on their websites to privacy/security matters than do non-OECD countries. Specifically, 91% of cities evaluated in OECD countries have developed a privacy or security statement/ policy, while only 48% of cities in non-OECD countries have a privacy statement on their websites. Both OECD and non-OECD countries show a rise in this number from 2013-14. Overall, 70% of cities had privacy/security statements, which was a 20% increase from 2013-14 at only 50%.

Table 5-4. *Results for Privacy and Security by OECD Member and Non-Member Countries (2015-16)*

	OECD	Average	Non-OECD
Privacy or Security Policy	91%	70%	48%
Use of Encryption	45%	29%	13%
Use of Cookies	76%	48%	20%
Digital Signature	18%	13%	8%

With regard to the use of encryption in the transmission of data, 45% of cities evaluated in OECD countries have a privacy policy addressing the use of encryption, compared to 13% of cities in non-OECD countries. Overall, 29% of cities addressed the use of encryption in their privacy/security statements, a rise of 7% from 22% in 2013-14. In addition, 76% of cities evaluated in OECD countries have a privacy policy addressing the use of "cookies" or "web beacons" to track users, while only 20% of cities in non-OECD countries have statements as to the use of "cookies." Both show increases in percentage from 2013-14. Overall, 41% of cities addressed the use of "cookies" in their privacy/security statements. Overall, cities in OECD countries score above average throughout the world.

In terms of queries and whether the site has a privacy or security statement/ policy, 70% of cities had privacy and security policies (Figure 5-3). Manama, Prague, Helsinki, Vilnius, and Oslo have clear privacy or security statements/ policies, as reflected by their rankings in that category.

Figure 5-3. *Existence of Privacy or Security Policy (2015-16)*

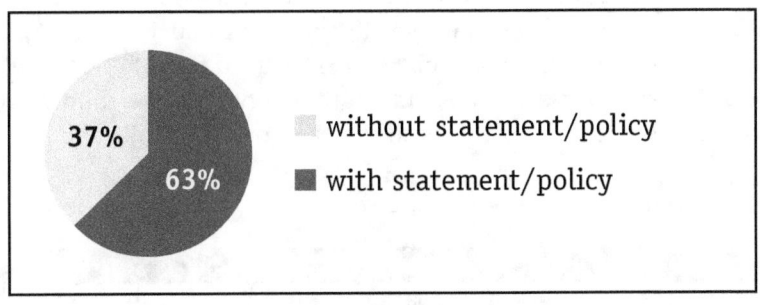

CHAPTER 6

Usability

The following chapter highlights the results for the category of Usability. Results indicate that Tokyo, Hong Kong, Yerevan, Helsinki and Tallinn are the top-ranked cities in the category of usability in 2015-16. Except for Yerevan, all 5 cities are new to the top-five rankings. Tokyo ranks first, with a score of 18.13 out of a maximum score of 20, showing a vast improvement from its position at 41st and score of 12.82 in 2013-14. Following is Hong Kong and Yerevan, with identical scores of 17.81 in the 2nd position. The fourth position is shared by Helsinki, and Tallinn, with scores of 17.50 each. Table 6-1 summarizes the results for all the municipalities evaluated in this category.

The average score in this category is 12.38, which is an overall increase from a score of 12.04 in 2013-14. The results indicate that cities in Oceana scored the highest in this category, with an overall score of 15.00 in Usability. Europe scored the second highest average of 13.27, similar to the 2013-14 results. Cities in Asia, however, replaced those in South America for the third place position, with an average score of 11.99 in the category of Usability.

Table 6-1. Results in Usability (2015-16)

Rank	City	Country	Usability
1	Tokyo	Japan	18.13
2	Hong Kong	China	17.81
2	Yerevan	Armenia	17.81
4	Helsinki	Finland	17.50
4	Tallinn	Estonia	17.50
6	Bratislava	Slovakia	17.19
7	Moscow	Russian Federation	16.88
8	Madrid	Spain	16.56
9	Buenos Aires	Argentina	16.25
10	Seoul	Korea (Rep.)	15.94
10	Sydney	Australia	15.94
10	Dubai	United Arab Emirates	15.94
13	Vilnius	Lithuania	15.63
14	Bucharest	Romania	15.31
14	Brussels	Belgium	15.31

Rank	City	Country	Usability
14	Luxembourg City	Luxembourg	15.31
14	Prague	Czech Republic	15.31
14	Stockholm	Sweden	15.31
14	Zurich	Switzerland	15.31
14	Kiev	Ukraine	15.31
14	Tbilisi	Georgia	15.31
22	Bogota	Colombia	15.00
22	London	United Kingdom	15.00
24	Toronto	Canada	14.69
24	Shanghai	China	14.69
26	Amsterdam	Netherlands	14.38
26	Singapore	Singapore	14.38
28	Johannesburg	South Africa	14.06
28	Auckland	New Zealand	14.06
28	New York	United States	14.06
28	Sarajevo	Bosnia and Herzegovina	14.06
28	Taipei	Taiwan, Province of China	14.06
33	Almaty	Kazakhstan	13.75
34	Copenhagen	Denmark	13.44
34	Muscat	Oman	13.44
34	Sana'a	Yemen	13.44
37	Guayaquil	Ecuador	13.13
37	Athens	Greece	13.13
37	Nicosia	Cyprus	13.13
40	Doha	Qatar	12.81
40	Berlin	Germany	12.81
40	Sao Paulo	Brazil	12.81
40	Tunis	Tunisia	12.81
40	Zagreb	Croatia	12.81
45	Belgrade	Serbia and Montenegro	12.50
45	Cairo	Egypt	12.50
45	Casablanca	Morocco	12.50
45	Dublin	Ireland	12.50
45	Istanbul	Turkey	12.50
45	Lisbon	Portugal	12.50
45	Santo Domingo	Dominican Republic	12.50
52	Montevideo	Uruguay	12.19
53	Amman	Jordan	11.88
53	Kuala Lumpur	Malaysia	11.88
53	Ljubljana	Slovenia	11.88
53	Mexico City	Mexico	11.88

continued

Rank	City	Country	Usability
53	Sofia	Bulgaria	11.88
58	Colombo	Sri Lanka	11.56
59	Delhi	India	11.25
59	Jakarta	Indonesia	11.25
59	Riga	Latvia	11.25
59	Jerusalem	Israel	11.25
63	Bangkok	Thailand	10.94
63	Chisinau	Moldova	10.94
63	Dhaka	Bangladesh	10.94
63	Kathmandu	Nepal	10.94
63	Oslo	Norway	10.94
63	Vienna	Austria	10.94
69	Karachi	Pakistan	10.63
69	Minsk	Belarus	10.63
69	Tirana	Albania	10.63
69	Budapest	Hungary	10.63
73	San Jose	Costa Rica	10.31
73	Warsaw	Poland	10.31
75	Bishkek	Kyrgyzstan	10.00
75	San Fernando	Trinidad & Tobago	10.00
75	Ulaanbaatar	Mongolia	10.00
75	Rome	Italy	10.00
79	Manama	Bahrain	9.69
79	San Juan	Puerto Rico	9.69
81	Port Louis	Mauritius	9.38
81	San Salvador	El Salvador	9.38
81	Tashkent	Uzbekistan	9.38
81	Tehran	Iran	9.38
85	Panama City	Panama	9.06
85	Paris	France	9.06
87	Addis Ababa	Ethiopia	8.44
87	Santiago	Chile	8.44
89	Skopje	Macedonia	8.13
90	Guatemala City	Guatemala	7.81
90	Ho Chi Minh	Vietnam	7.81
90	Riyadh	Saudi Arabia	7.81
93	Baku	Azerbaijan	7.50
93	Caracas	Venezuela	7.50
93	Gaza	Palestine	7.50
96	Lima	Peru	6.88
97	Manila	Philippines	6.56

Table 6-2 represents the average scores in Usability grouped by continent. Overall, cities in Oceania scored the highest in usability with an average score of 15.00. Europe scored the second highest average of 13.27, while cities in North America scored the lowest average of 11.04 in this category.

As shown in Figure 6-2, cities in OECD countries scored an average of 13.63, while cities in non-member countries scored only 11.74 in this category. This result indicates that cities in economically advanced countries continue to have more emphasis on usability than do cities in less developed countries. The gap between OECD member and non-member countries has remained largely the same as in the 2013-14 survey, but both member and non-member countries have increased their average Usability score. Figure 6-1 summarizes the data presented in Table 6-2.

Table 6-2. *Average Score in Usability by Continent (2015-16)*

	Oceania	Europe	Asia	Average	North America	South America	Africa
Usability Averages	15	13.27	11.99	12.38	11.04	11.35	11.61

Figure 6-1. *Average Score in Usability by Continent (2015-16)*

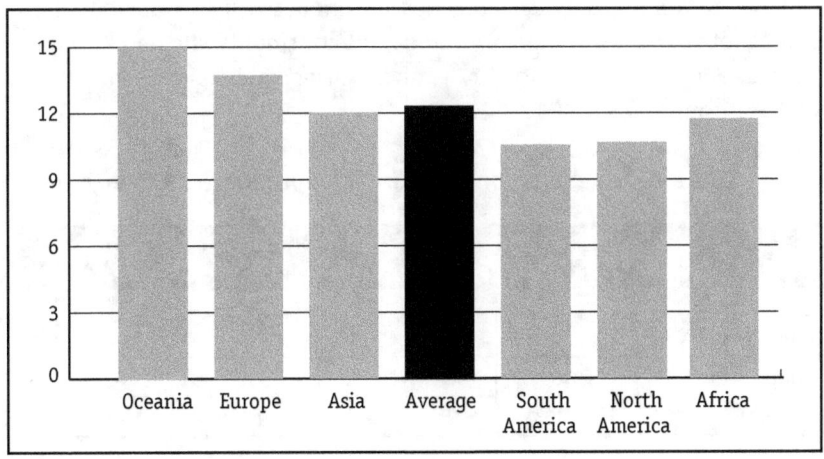

Figure 6-2. *Average Score in Usability by OECD Member and Non-Member Countries (2015-16)*

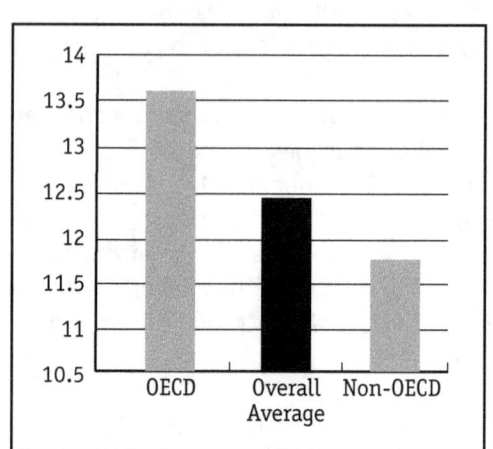

Table 6-3 lists the results of the evaluation of key aspects in the category of Usability by continent. Oceania remained at 100% with regard to targeted audience links. This was followed by 89% of cities in North America, 71% of cities in Europe, 67% of cities in South America, 67% of cities in Asia, and 67% of cities in Africa that have targeted audience links divided into more than three categories (e.g., general citizens, youth, the elderly, women, family, citizens in need of social welfare services, businesses, industry, small businesses, public employees, etc.). Save for South America, all continents showed an increase in their score. Further, on average, 77% of all cities that have such links show a rise of 15% from 62% in 2013-14.

Table 6-3. *Results for Usability by Continent (2015-16)*

	Oceania	Europe	Asia	Average	North America	South America	Africa
Targeted Audience	100%	71%	67%	77%	89%	67%	67%
Site map	50%	66%	67%	58%	56%	44%	67%
Search tool	100%	100%	94%	99%	100%	100%	100%

Also, as to the posting of site maps that contain active links and are less than two screens in length, Asia and Africa have the highest scores with 67%, followed by 66% in Europe, 56% in North America, 50%in Oceania, and 44% in South America. Save for Africa, the increase in percentage of site maps was non-existent or slight among the continents. Overall, 58% of cities had a site map that contained active links and are less than two screens in length, a drop of 3% from 61% in 2013-14. In terms of online search tools, all cities in Oceania, Europe, South America, and Africa contained a search tool. Asia had a search tool available for 94% of websites. All cities showed a rise in their percentages, with near all continents reaching 100% in terms of this feature.

Table 6-3. *Results for Usability by Continent (2015-16)*

	Oceania	Europe	Asia	Average	North America	South America	Africa
Targeted Audience	100%	71%	67%	77%	89%	67%	67%
Site map	50%	66%	67%	58%	56%	44%	67%
Search tool	100%	100%	94%	99%	100%	100%	100%

Table 6-4 indicates the results of assessments of Usability among OECD and non-OECD countries. In terms of targeted audience links, 74% of cities throughout the world have targeted audience links divided into more than three categories. Further, 85% of cities in OECD countries have links divided into more than three categories, while only 64% of non-OECD countries have such links. Both showed a rise in the overall average, however.

With regard to sitemaps, 64% of cities throughout the world have a sitemap containing active links and are less than two screens in length. This was a drop of 7% from 71% in 2013-14. Also, 67% of the cities in OECD countries and 61% in non-OECD countries contained a sitemap. This shows a drop in OECD countries, and a rise in non-OECD countries since 2013-14.

Lastly, 100% of the cities in OECD countries and 97% in non-OECD countries provide online search tools. Both showed increases in scores since 2013-14. The average score among cities throughout the world was 98%.

Table 6-4. *Results for Usability by OECD Member and Non-Member Countries (2015-16)*

	OECD	Average	Non-OECD
Targeted Audience	75%	62%	54%
Site map	71%	61%	56%
Search tool	97%	90%	86%

In terms of the topic of "Targeted audience links: Are targeted audience links available on the homepage?" (e.g., general citizens, youth, the elderly, women, citizens in need of social welfare services, businesses, industry, public employees, etc.), 74% of municipal websites are divided into more than three categories (Figure 6-3).

Figure 6-3. *Targeted Audience Links (2015-16)*

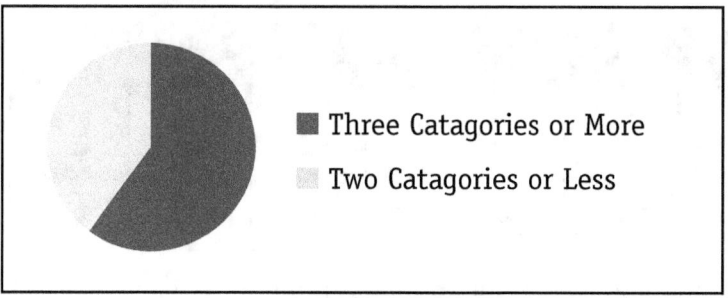

CHAPTER 7

Content

Results for the category of content indicate that Seoul, New York, Madrid, Prague, and Yerevan are the top-ranked cities in this category. New to the top five are Madrid and Prague. Seoul remained in the 1st place position in content, with a score of 17.30, relatively similar to its 2013-14 score. New York was ranked 5th in 2013-14, but it has improved to second overall, with a score of 15.71 in 2015-16. Table 7-1 summarizes the results for all the municipalities evaluated in the content category. Madrid was ranked 43rd in 2013-14 with a score of 7.94, but has changed its score significantly to 15.56 in 2015-16. Similarly, Prague was ranked 26th respectively in 2013-14 with a score of 9.84, but is now ranked 4th with a score of 15.08. Yerevan dropped one position to fifth in 2015-16, from its fourth place position in 2013-14, having an unchanged score of 14.92.

The average score for the top-five-ranked cities in 2015-16 is 8.22. This shows an increase in the overall average content score for this category from 7.62 in 2013-14.

Table 7-1. *Results for Content (2015-16)*

Rank	City	Country	Content
1	Seoul	Korea (Rep.)	17.30
2	New York	United States	15.71
3	Madrid	Spain	15.56
4	Prague	Czech Republic	15.08
5	Yerevan	Armenia	14.92
6	Oslo	Norway	14.44
7	Tallinn	Estonia	14.13
8	Bratislava	Slovakia	13.97
8	Moscow	Russian Federation	13.97
8	Bogota	Colombia	13.97
11	Zurich	Switzerland	13.81
11	Ljubljana	Slovenia	13.81
13	Hong Kong	China	13.65
14	Helsinki	Finland	13.17

continued

Rank	City	Country	Content
15	Stockholm	Sweden	13.02
16	Amsterdam	Netherlands	12.86
17	Vienna	Austria	12.70
18	Tokyo	Japan	12.54
19	Vilnius	Lithuania	12.22
19	Auckland	New Zealand	12.22
21	Jerusalem	Israel	12.06
22	Toronto	Canada	11.90
22	Lisbon	Portugal	11.90
24	Istanbul	Turkey	11.59
25	Copenhagen	Denmark	11.27
26	Mexico City	Mexico	11.11
27	Rome	Italy	10.95
28	Johannesburg	South Africa	10.63
29	Kiev	Ukraine	10.32
29	Kuala Lumpur	Malaysia	10.32
31	Sydney	Australia	10.16
31	Singapore	Singapore	10.16
33	Buenos Aires	Argentina	10.00
33	London	United Kingdom	10.00
35	Sao Paulo	Brazil	9.84
36	Berlin	Germany	9.84
37	Paris	France	9.68
38	Ulaanbaatar	Mongolia	9.52
39	Riga	Latvia	9.05
40	Sarajevo	Bosnia and Herzegovina	8.73
41	Zagreb	Croatia	8.57
41	Budapest	Hungary	8.57
43	San Salvador	El Salvador	8.25
44	Santo Domingo	Dominican Republic	8.10
45	Delhi	India	7.94
45	Jakarta	Indonesia	7.94
47	Taipei	Taiwan, Province of China	7.78
48	Shanghai	China	7.78
49	Belgrade	Serbia and Montenegro	7.46
50	Brussels	Belgium	7.46
51	Luxembourg City	Luxembourg	7.30
52	Dublin	Ireland	7.30
52	Santiago	Chile	7.30
54	Tbilisi	Georgia	7.14
54	San Jose	Costa Rica	7.14
56	Dubai	United Arab Emirates	6.67

Rank	City	Country	Content
56	Tehran	Iran	6.67
58	Athens	Greece	6.51
58	Panama City	Panama	6.51
58	Lima	Peru	6.51
61	Montevideo	Uruguay	6.19
62	Bucharest	Romania	5.87
63	Sofia	Bulgaria	5.56
64	Nicosia	Cyprus	5.40
64	Amman	Jordan	5.40
66	Ho Chi Minh	Vietnam	5.40
67	Cairo	Egypt	5.24
67	Bishkek	Kyrgyzstan	5.24
69	San Fernando	Trinidad & Tobago	5.08
69	Riyadh	Saudi Arabia	5.08
71	Doha	Qatar	4.92
71	Caracas	Venezuela	4.92
73	Karachi	Pakistan	4.76
73	Tashkent	Uzbekistan	4.76
73	Skopje	Macedonia	4.76
76	Manama	Bahrain	4.60
77	Almaty	Kazakhstan	4.44
77	Chisinau	Moldova	4.44
79	Muscat	Oman	4.29
79	Casablanca	Morocco	4.29
79	Minsk	Belarus	4.29
79	Warsaw	Poland	4.29
79	Guatemala City	Guatemala	4.29
84	Colombo	Sri Lanka	4.13
84	Tirana	Albania	4.13
84	San Juan	Puerto Rico	4.13
87	Dhaka	Bangladesh	4.05
88	Guayaquil	Ecuador	3.97
88	Port Louis	Mauritius	3.97
90	Bangkok	Thailand	3.81
90	Kathmandu	Nepal	3.81
92	Tunis	Tunisia	3.65
93	Gaza	Palestine	2.38
94	Baku	Azerbaijan	2.38
95	Manila	Philippines	2.22
96	Sana'a	Yemen	2.06
96	Addis Ababa	Ethiopia	2.06

Table 7-2 represents the average score in Content by continent. Overall, cities in Oceania had the highest average score of 11.19, and Oceania remained the highest rated continent. Africa, however, remained the continent with the lowest average, with a score of 4.97. As shown in Figure 7-2, cities in OECD countries scored an average of 11.5, while cities in non-member countries scored only 6.53 in this category. Cities in economically advanced countries continue to have more emphasis on website content than do cities in less developed countries. Once again, however, both OECD member and non-member countries increased their overall Content scores. Figure 7-1 illustrates the data presented in Table 7-2.

Table 7-2. *Average Score in Content by Continent (2015-16)*

	Oceania	Europe	Asia	Average	North America	South America	Africa
Content Averages	11.19	9.84	6.85	8.22	8.57	7.53	4.97

Figure 7-1. *Average Score in Content by Continent (2015-16)*

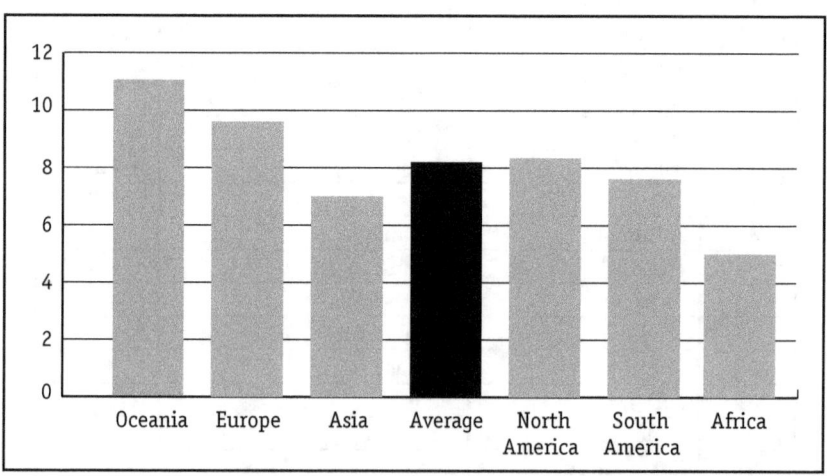

Table 7-3 indicates the results of the evaluation of Content by continent. First, 52% of cities evaluated in Oceania, Europe, and Asia have websites with performance measurement mechanisms posted throughout the website. Next, 53% of cities evaluated in Oceania, Europe, and Asia have websites with mechanisms in the area of emergency management or alerts (severe weather, etc.). This shows a significant rise from the level of 35% in 2013-14.

Figure 7-2. *Average Score in Content by OECD Member and Non-Member Countries (2015-16)*

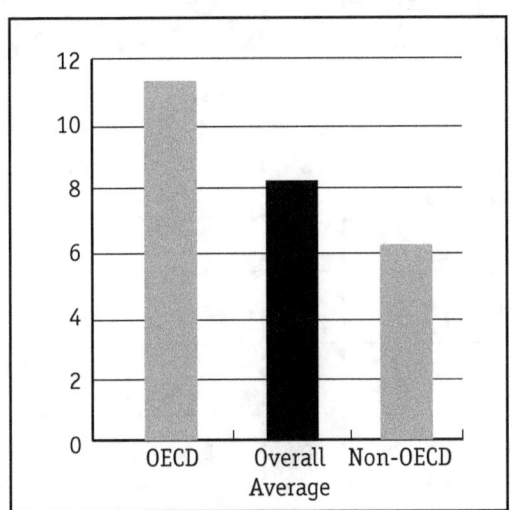

Subsequently, with regard to disability access for the blind, 34% of cites have websites providing such access (e.g., Bobby compliant: http://www.cast.org/bobby). This shows a 23% rise from the 2013-14 score of 11%. In addition, 26% of cities have websites providing disability access for the deaf (TDD phone service).

Among continents, cities in Oceania have the highest percentage—50% of municipal websites with both blind- and deaf-assistance features. Cities in Africa have no websites providing disability access for the blind or for the deaf.

Regarding the use of wireless technology, 33% of cities in Asia and North America, 32% of cities in Europe, 22% of cities in South America, and 17% of cities in Africa have websites using such technology, such as messages to a mobile phone or PDA (Personal Digital Assistant) to update applications, events, etc. No cities in Oceania have websites using this technology. All cities showed a rise in this category, except those in Oceania. Overall, 23% of websites contained this feature.

Also, 89% of cities in Europe, 85% of cities in Asia, 67% of cities in Africa, 56% of cities in North America, 50% of cities in Oceania, and 33% of cities in South America have websites offering access in more than one language. All cities showed a rise in this category, except those in Oceania. Overall, 63% of websites offered access in multiple languages.

Table 7-3. *Results for Content by Continent (2015-16)*

	Oceania	Europe	Asia	Average	North America	South America	Africa
Emergency Management	100%	61%	58%	53%	56%	44%	0%
Access for the Blind	50%	47%	18%	34%	44%	44%	0%
Access for the deaf	50%	34%	18%	26%	22%	33%	0%
Wireless technology	0%	32%	33%	23%	33%	22%	17%
More than one language	50%	89%	85%	63%	56%	33%	67%
Performance Measurement	100%	53%	30%	52%	56%	56%	17%

Table 7-4 indicates the results of assessments of Content among OECD and non-OECD countries. As with the other categories discussed above, cities in OECD countries have more advanced websites in terms of content than do cities in non-OECD countries. Of note, the overall averages have risen among both OECD and non-OECD countries. Regarding performance measurement, 70% of OECD counties have performance measurements posted on their websites, while only 31% of non-OECD countries do. As to an emergency management or an alert mechanism, 76% of cities in OECD countries have such websites, but only 44% of cities in non-OECD member countries have such capacities.

In terms of disability access for the blind, 67% of cities in OECD countries have websites providing such access, whereas only 17% of cities in non-OECD countries offer that capacity. In addition, 48% of cities in OECD countries have websites providing disability access for the deaf, while only 14% of cities in non-OECD countries offer it. With respect to the use of wireless technology, 48% of cities in OECD countries have websites using wireless technology to update applications, events, etc., while only 20% of cities in non-OECD countries have websites using that technology. Lastly, 91% of cities in OECD countries have websites offering access in more than one language, while 70% in non-OECD countries offer multilingual access. Universally, the averages have risen since 2013-14, but the gap in content between OECD and Non-OECD countries is characteristically still present in 2015-16.

Table 7-4. *Results for Content by OECD Member and Non-Member Countries (2015-16)*

	OECD	Average	Non-OECD
Emergency Management	76%	60%	44%
Access for the blind	67%	42%	17%
Access for the deaf	48%	31%	14%
Use of wireless technology	48%	34%	20%
More than one language	91%	81%	70%
Performance Measurement	70%	50%	31%

We asked: "Does the site offer access in more than one language?" Some 81% of cities evaluated have a website that offers access in more than one language, while 19% of cities have access in only one language. Figure 7-3 represents these findings in terms of overall percentages. This is a drastic increase from the overall average of only 55% of websites having access in multiple languages in 2013-14.

Figure 7-3. *Access in Multiple Languages (2015-16)*

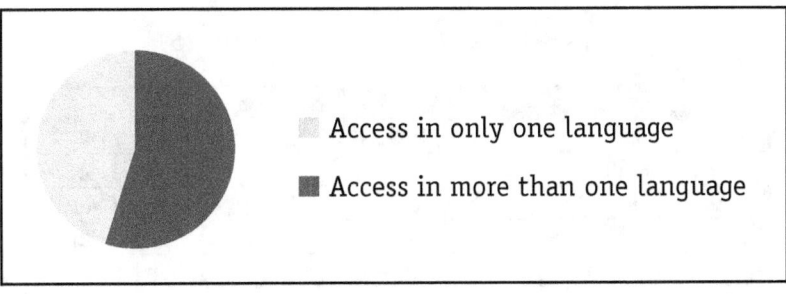

Access in only one language

Access in more than one language

CHAPTER 8

Services

The following chapter highlights the results for the category of online services. Results indicate that Seoul, Tallinn, Hong Kong, Jerusalem, and New York are the top-ranked cities in the category of online services. Seoul remained in the first position with a score of 16.89 out of a maximum score of 20. In second place was Tallinn, with a score of 15.08, moving up from its 20th position and score of 8.36. Hong Kong is ranked third, with a score of 14.75, a jump from its fifth place position and score of 12.79 in 2013-14. Jerusalem ranked fourth, with a score of 13.61, which showed a large jump from its score of 7.22 in 2013-14. The fifth ranked city is New York, with a score of 13.61, dropping from its third-place position in 2013-14 and score of 15.25. Table 8-1 summarizes the results for all municipalities evaluated in this category.

The average score in the service category is 6.82 in 2015-16. This shows an overall increase from cities' scores of 5.49 in 2013-14.

Table 8-1. *Results in Services (2015-16)*

Rank	City	Country	Content
1	Seoul	Korea (Rep.)	16.89
2	Tallinn	Estonia	15.08
3	Hong Kong	China	14.75
4	Jerusalem	Israel	13.61
5	New York	United States	13.61
6	Madrid	Spain	13.44
7	Tokyo	Japan	13.11
7	Singapore	Singapore	13.11
9	Mexico City	Mexico	12.95
10	Bogota	Colombia	12.46
11	Yerevan	Armenia	12.13
11	Moscow	Russian Federation	12.13
13	Amsterdam	Netherlands	11.97
14	Helsinki	Finland	11.80
15	Auckland	New Zealand	11.80
16	Prague	Czech Republic	11.64
17	Istanbul	Turkey	11.15

Rank	City	City	Content
17	London	United Kingdom	11.15
19	Copenhagen	Denmark	10.98
20	Buenos Aires	Argentina	10.82
21	Oslo	Norway	10.33
22	Vilnius	Lithuania	10.16
23	Sydney	Australia	10.00
24	Sao Paulo	Brazil	9.84
25	Dubai	United Arab Emirates	9.67
26	Ljubljana	Slovenia	9.34
27	Toronto	Canada	9.34
28	Lisbon	Portugal	8.85
29	Zagreb	Croatia	8.69
30	Rome	Italy	8.36
30	Riga	Latvia	8.36
30	Tbilisi	Georgia	8.36
30	Athens	Greece	8.36
30	Manama	Bahrain	8.36
35	Kuala Lumpur	Malaysia	8.20
35	Berlin	Germany	8.20
35	Shanghai	China	8.20
38	Paris	France	8.20
38	Delhi	India	8.20
38	Nicosia	Cyprus	8.20
41	Zurich	Switzerland	8.03
41	Taipei	Taiwan, Province of China	8.03
41	Dublin	Ireland	8.03
44	Stockholm	Sweden	7.70
45	San Jose	Costa Rica	7.54
46	Bratislava	Slovakia	7.54
47	Johannesburg	South Africa	7.38
48	Brussels	Belgium	7.05
48	Tehran	Iran	7.05
48	Almaty	Kazakhstan	7.05
51	Sarajevo	Bosnia and Herzegovina	6.89
52	Doha	Qatar	6.72
53	Muscat	Oman	5.90
53	San Juan	Puerto Rico	5.90
55	Montevideo	Uruguay	4.92
56	Kiev	Ukraine	4.75
57	Santo Domingo	Dominican Republic	4.75
57	Tashkent	Uzbekistan	4.75

continued

Rank	City	Country	Content
59	Luxembourg City	Luxembourg	4.43
59	Amman	Jordan	4.43
59	Caracas	Venezuela	4.43
59	Colombo	Sri Lanka	4.43
63	Vienna	Austria	4.26
64	Belgrade	Serbia and Montenegro	4.10
65	Budapest	Hungary	4.10
66	San Salvador	El Salvador	3.77
66	Jakarta	Indonesia	3.77
66	Port Louis	Mauritius	3.77
69	Dhaka	Bangladesh	3.61
70	Casablanca	Morocco	3.44
70	Kathmandu	Nepal	3.44
72	Cairo	Egypt	3.28
73	Ulaanbaatar	Mongolia	3.11
73	San Fernando	Trinidad & Tobago	3.11
73	Karachi	Pakistan	3.11
76	Guatemala City	Guatemala	3.11
77	Minsk	Belarus	3.11
78	Panama City	Panama	2.95
78	Sofia	Bulgaria	2.95
80	Bucharest	Romania	2.79
80	Ho Chi Minh	Vietnam	2.79
80	Gaza	Palestine	2.79
83	Chisinau	Moldova	2.62
83	Manila	Philippines	2.62
85	Skopje	Macedonia	2.30
86	Bishkek	Kyrgyzstan	2.13
86	Guayaquil	Ecuador	2.13
88	Warsaw	Poland	2.13
89	Bangkok	Thailand	1.97
89	Tunis	Tunisia	1.97
91	Riyadh	Saudi Arabia	1.80
92	Lima	Peru	1.48
93	Addis Ababa	Ethiopia	1.31
94	Tirana	Albania	0.98
95	Santiago	Chile	0.82
96	Sana'a	Yemen	0.66
97	Baku	Azerbaijan	0.00

Table 8-2 represents the average score of online services by continent. Overall, cities in Oceania again ranked highest, with a score of 10.9, followed by European cities, which remained in the second position with a score of 7.64. North American cities ranked third, with a score of 7.1, while cities in Asia ranked fourth, with a score of 6.51.

Further, cities in OECD countries had an average score of 9.52 in 2015-16, a large increase in their average score of 7.70 from 2013-14. Conversely, cities in non-member countries recorded an average of 5.43 in this category, which was also an increase in the average service score of 4.40 from 2013-14. This result suggests that cities in developed countries have provided citizens with more online services than cities in less developed countries. Figures 8-1 and 8-2 highlight that conclusion.

Table 8-2. *Average Score in Services by Continent (2015-16)*

	Oceania	Europe	Asia	Average	North America	South America	Africa
Service Averages	10.9	7.64	6.51	6.82	7.1	5.56	3.52

Figure 8-1. *Average Score in Services by Continent (2015-16)*

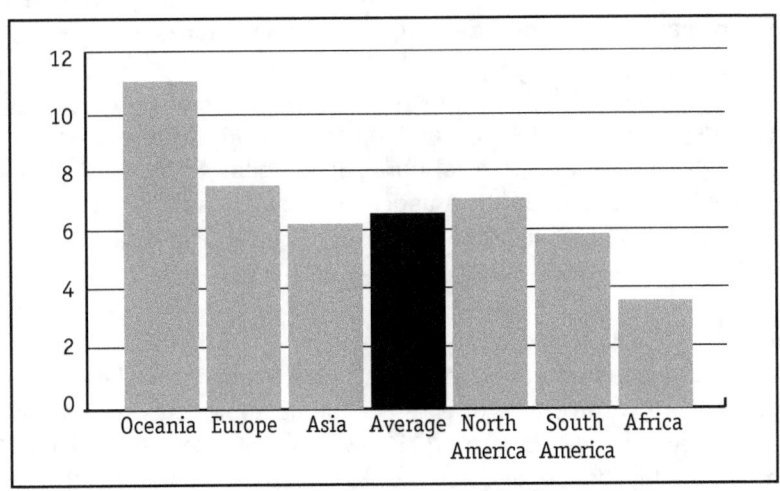

Figure 8-2. *Average Score in Services by OECD Member and Non-Member Countries (2015-16)*

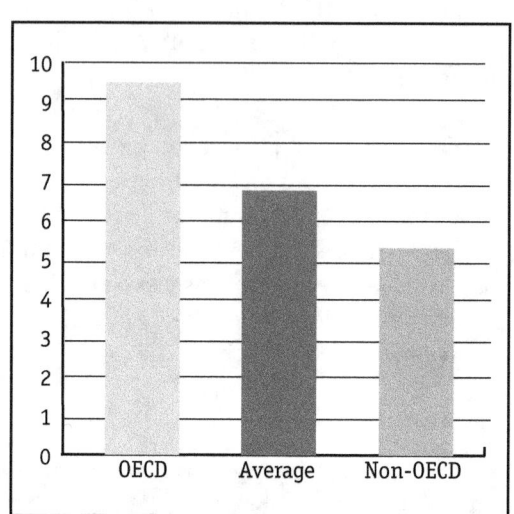

Table 8-3 indicates the results of key aspects selected in the category of service delivery by continent. With regard to searchable databases, 100% of cities in Oceania, 78% of cities in South America, 76% in Europe, 67% in Asia, 44% in North America, and 17% in Africa have websites offering a searchable database. All continents, save for Africa which dropped 12%, showed an increase in this score. The overall average for cities with searchable databases was 64%.

In terms of portal customization, which allows users to customize the main city homepage, depending on their needs, percentages are far lower. Asia had the highest degree of portal customization at 30%, followed by North America at 22%, Europe at 18%, and South America at 11%. Oceania and Africa had no websites with portal customization. The overall percentage rose 4%, to 14% in 2015-16 from 10% in 2013-14.

In addition, with respect to access to their private information online (e.g., educational records, medical records, point total of driving violations, lost pet dogs, lost property), some 29% of cities in Europe allow users such access. This was an increase of 11% from the 2013-14 score of 19%. Specifically, South America had the highest degree of access to private information online at 56%, followed by North America at 44%, Europe at 32%, Asia at 24%, and Africa at 17%. Oceania had no access to such records. As represented by the overall average of 18%, all cities showed significant increases in such access since 2013-14.

Table 8-3. *Results for Services by Continent (2015-16)*

	Oceania	Europe	Asia	Average	North America	South America	Africa
Searchable Database	100%	76%	67%	64%	44%	78%	17%
Portal Customization	0%	18%	30%	14%	22%	11%	0%
Access to Private Info	0%	32%	24%	29%	44%	56%	17%

Table 8-4 represents the results of key aspects in the category of service delivery by OECD membership. With regard to searchable databases, 91% of cities in OECD countries have websites offering a searchable database, and 55% in non-OECD countries have sites offering that capacity. In terms of portal customization, 33% of cities in OECD countries allow users to customize the main city homepage depending on their needs, and 14% in non-OECD countries allow citizens to do so. In addition, with respect to access to private information online, 45% of cities in OECD countries allow users to access such information, while 23% of cities in non-OECD countries allow citizens to do so. Among all categories, there was a rise in percentage among both OECD and Non-OECD countries since 2013-14.

Table 8-4. *Results for Services by OECD Member and Non-Member Countries (2015-16)*

	OECD	Average	Non-OECD
Searchable Database	91%	73%	55%
Portal Customization	33%	24%	14%
Access Private Info	45%	34%	23%

Overall, 29% of all cities allow citizens access to their private information online in response to the question, "Does the site allow access to private information online?" (e.g., educational records, medical records, point total of driving violations, lost pet dogs, lost property). Over 71% of cities do not allow such access. Though there has been a rise in such access since 2013-14, where only 18% of cities provided such access, the gap is still large. Figure 8-3 (see next page) illustrates this finding.

Figure 8-3. *Access to Private Information Online (2015-16)*

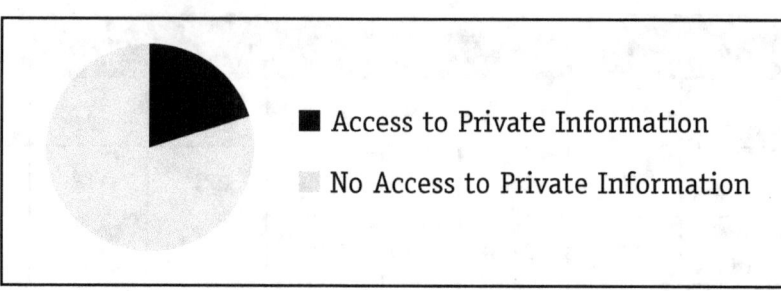

CHAPTER 9

Citizen and Social Engagement

The following chapter highlights the results for the category of citizen and social engagement. Results indicate that Seoul, Helsinki, Madrid, Yerevan, and Prague are the top-ranked cities in the category of citizen and social engagement. New to the top five are Helsinki, Madrid, and Prague. Seoul ranked first again, with a score of 16.46, but dropped in score compared to its score of 18.75 in 2013-14. Helsinki, which ranked 11th in 2013-14 and had a score of 7.29, was in the second position in 2015-16, with a score of 12.92. Madrid made staggering progress in this category, from its ranking of 68th in 2013-14 with score of 1.25 to the third position in 2015-16 with a score of 11.46. Yerevan came in at the fourth ranking, with a score of 11.04, the same score it achieved in 2013-14. It was followed by Prague, with a score of 10.00, a jump from 16th position and a score of 5.83 in 2013-14. Table 9-1 summarizes the results for all municipalities evaluated in this category.

The average score in this category is 3.87, which shows a slight increase from a score of 3.34 in 2013-14. Overall, cities have been slow in developing e-governance outlets that would empower citizen participation. This can be attributed to the relative lack of support for online citizen participation outlets and practices among municipalities across the world.

Table 9-1. *Results in Citizen and Social Engagement (2015-16)*

Rank	City	Country	Content
1	Seoul	Korea (Rep.)	16.46
2	Helsinki	Finland	12.92
3	Madrid	Spain	11.46
4	Yerevan	Armenia	11.04
5	Prague	Czech Republic	10.00
6	Bratislava	Slovakia	9.79
7	Moscow	Russian Federation	9.17
7	Lisbon	Portugal	9.17
9	Buenos Aires	Argentina	8.96

continued

Rank	City	Country	Content
10	Hong Kong	China	8.75
10	Singapore	Singapore	8.75
10	Shanghai	China	8.75
13	Auckland	New Zealand	7.29
14	Paris	France	7.08
15	Manama	Bahrain	7.08
16	Tallinn	Estonia	6.88
17	Vilnius	Lithuania	6.67
18	Berlin	Germany	6.25
18	Tehran	Iran	6.25
20	New York	United States	6.04
20	Dublin	Ireland	6.04
22	Sydney	Australia	5.83
23	Mexico City	Mexico	5.63
24	Zurich	Switzerland	5.42
24	Minsk	Belarus	5.42
26	Ljubljana	Slovenia	5.42
27	Copenhagen	Denmark	5.21
28	Bogota	Colombia	5.00
28	Stockholm	Sweden	5.00
28	Sarajevo	Bosnia and Herzegovina	5.00
28	Vienna	Austria	5.00
32	Amsterdam	Netherlands	4.79
33	Oslo	Norway	4.58
33	Toronto	Canada	4.58
33	Santo Domingo	Dominican Republic	4.58
36	Luxembourg City	Luxembourg	4.58
37	Tokyo	Japan	4.38
37	Tbilisi	Georgia	4.38
39	Jerusalem	Israel	4.17
39	Istanbul	Turkey	4.17
41	London	United Kingdom	4.17
42	Kuala Lumpur	Malaysia	3.75
42	Nicosia	Cyprus	3.75
42	Kiev	Ukraine	3.75
45	Johannesburg	South Africa	3.54
46	Taipei	Taiwan, Province of China	3.54
46	Amman	Jordan	3.54
48	Zagreb	Croatia	3.33
48	Muscat	Oman	3.33
50	Almaty	Kazakhstan	3.13
50	Bucharest	Romania	3.13
52	Athens	Greece	2.92
53	Tashkent	Uzbekistan	2.71

Rank	City	Country	Content
54	Chisinau	Moldova	2.50
55	Sao Paulo	Brazil	2.29
55	Brussels	Belgium	2.29
57	San Jose	Costa Rica	2.08
58	Skopje	Macedonia	2.08
59	Delhi	India	1.88
59	Colombo	Sri Lanka	1.88
59	Belgrade	Serbia and Montenegro	1.88
59	Budapest	Hungary	1.88
63	Rome	Italy	1.67
63	San Fernando	Trinidad & Tobago	1.67
63	Riyadh	Saudi Arabia	1.67
66	Riga	Latvia	1.67
66	Montevideo	Uruguay	1.67
66	Jakarta	Indonesia	1.67
69	Port Louis	Mauritius	1.46
69	Karachi	Pakistan	1.46
71	Doha	Qatar	1.46
71	Kathmandu	Nepal	1.46
71	Panama City	Panama	1.46
71	Sofia	Bulgaria	1.46
75	Bishkek	Kyrgyzstan	1.25
75	Warsaw	Poland	1.25
75	Tunis	Tunisia	1.25
78	Ulaanbaatar	Mongolia	1.04
78	Lima	Peru	1.04
80	San Salvador	El Salvador	1.04
80	Dhaka	Bangladesh	1.04
82	Dubai	United Arab Emirates	0.83
82	Caracas	Venezuela	0.83
82	Cairo	Egypt	0.83
82	Manila	Philippines	0.83
82	Guayaquil	Ecuador	0.83
87	San Juan	Puerto Rico	0.63
87	Guatemala City	Guatemala	0.63
89	Ho Chi Minh	Vietnam	0.42
89	Gaza	Palestine	0.42
89	Bangkok	Thailand	0.42
89	Sana'a	Yemen	0.42
93	Casablanca	Morocco	0.21
93	Baku	Azerbaijan	0.21
95	Addis Ababa	Ethiopia	0.00
95	Tirana	Albania	0.00
95	Santiago	Chile	0.00

Table 9-2 represents the average score by continent. Overall, cities in Oceania replaced Asia as the highest ranked continent, with a score of 6.56. Europe garnered the second place position with a score of 4.94, and Asia the third position with a score of 3.59, a slight drop from the score of 3.99 in 2013-14.

As shown in Figure 9-2, cities in OECD countries scored an average of 5.83, which was a slight increase in their 2013-14 score of 5.12. Cities in non-member countries scored only 2.86 in this category, which shows a noticeable gap between member and non-member countries. This result indicates that cities in economically advanced countries continue to place more emphasis on citizen participation than do cities in less developed countries. Figures 9-1 illustrates the data presented in Table 9-2.

Table 9-2. *Average Score in Citizen and Social Engagement by Continent (2015-16)*

	Oceania	Europe	Asia	Average	North America	South America	Africa
CS Engagement Averages	6.56	4.94	3.59	3.87	2.96	2.48	1.22

Figure 9-1. *Average Score in Citizen and Social Engagement by Continent (2015-16)*

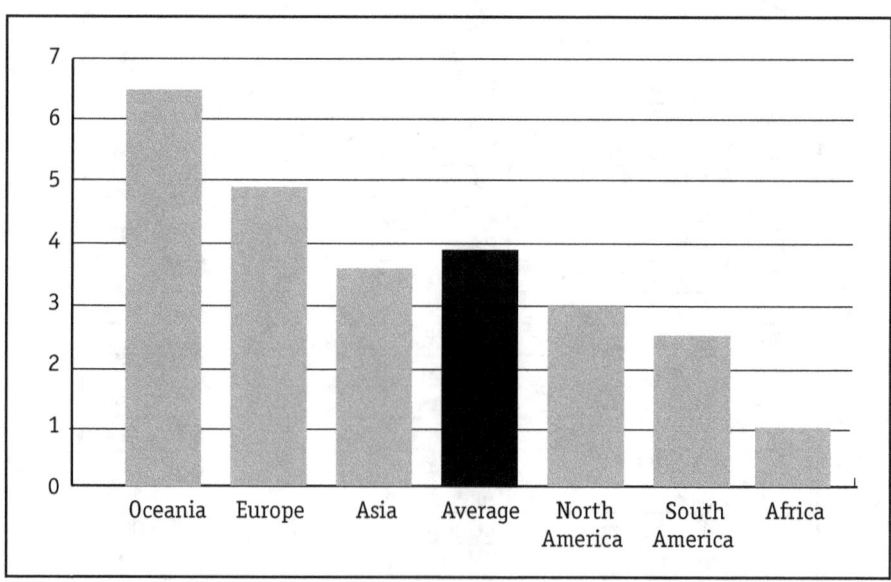

Figure 9-2. *Average Score in Citizen and Social Engagement by OECD Member and Non-Member Countries (2015-16)*

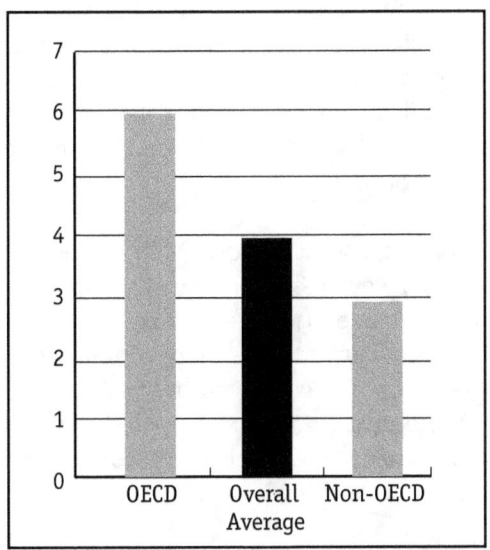

Table 9-3 indicates the results of key aspects of the category of Citizen and Social Engagement by continent. In terms of the evaluation to the question, "Does the website allow users to provide comments or feedback to individual departments/agencies through online forms?" 82% of municipalities do provide a mechanism allowing comments or feedback through such forms. This indicates a rather large increase from the average score of 60% in 2013-14. 100% of cities in Oceania offered access to such feedback forms, along with 87% of cities in Europe, 85% in Asia, 78% in North and South America, and 67% in Africa.

Table 9-3. *Results for Citizen and Social Engagement by Continent (2015-16)*

	Oceania	Europe	Asia	Average	North America	South America	Africa
Feedback Form	100%	87%	85%	82%	78%	78%	67%
Bulletin Board	0%	50%	36%	22%	11%	33%	0%
Policy Forum	50%	50%	27%	30%	11%	22%	17%

With respect to access to online bulletin board or chat capabilities for gathering citizen input on public issues ("online bulletin board" or "chat capabilities" refers to a city website where any citizens can post ideas, comments, or opinions without specific discussion topics), 22% of cities have these capabilities. This shows a 2% drop from the 2013-14 score of 24%. 50% of cities in Europe offered access to such bulletin boards, along with 36% of cities in Asia, 33% in South America, and 11% in North America. No cities in Oceania or Africa had access to bulletin boards of this sort.

Lastly, with regard to online discussion forums on policy issues ("online discussion forum" means the city websites where the city arranges public consultation on policy issues, and citizens participate in discussing those specific topics), 30% of the municipalities evaluated have a site containing an online discussion forum. This is an increase of 10% compared to the 2013-14 score of 20%. 50% of cities in Oceania offered access to such feedback forms, along with 30% of cities in Asia, 23% in Europe. 10% of cities in North and South America and Africa had access to such discussion forums.

Table 9-4 represents the results of key aspects selected in the category of Citizen and Social Engagement across OECD and non-OECD countries. In terms of the question, "Does the website allow users to provide comments or feedback to individual departments/agencies through online forms?," we found that 91 % of municipalities in OECD countries provide a mechanism allowing comments or feedback through online forms compared to 80% of municipalities in non-OECD countries. Overall, 85% of countries provide this mechanism of communication.

With respect to online bulletin board or chat capabilities for gathering citizen input on public issues, 45% of municipalities in OECD countries provide online bulletin board or chat capabilities, while 31% of municipalities in non-OECD countries provide such capabilities. Overall, 38% of countries provide this mechanism of communication.

With regard to online discussion forums on policy issues, 55% of municipalities in OECD countries have a site containing an online discussion forum, but only 23% of municipalities in non-OECD countries have a site containing such a forum. Similar to other categories, the percent of countries with these services has increased, but there is still a noticeable gap between OECD and non-OECD countries. Overall, 39% of countries provide this mechanism of communication.

Table 9-4. *Results for Citizen and Social Engagement by OECD Member and Non-Member Countries (2015-16)*

	OECD	Average	Non-OECD
Feedback Form	91%	85%	80%
Bulletin Board	45%	38%	31%
Policy Forum	55%	39%	23%

Figure 9-3. *Online Policy Forums (2015-16)*

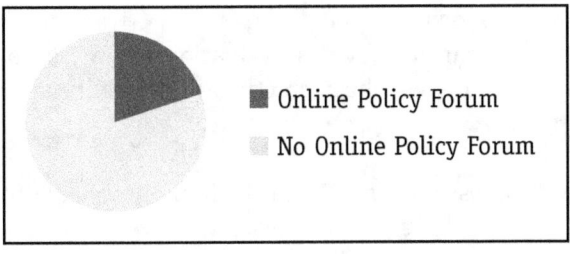

CHAPTER 10

Best Practices

Seoul

Seoul is again ranked #1 in the seventh Worldwide Digital Governance Survey. Across all dimensions, the government website of Seoul is ranked #6 in Privacy and Security, #10 in Usability, #1 in Content, #1 in Service Delivery, and #1 in Citizen and Social Engagement. Though the rank in Privacy and Security, as well as Usability, is lower than in previous evaluation results, on average Seoul is still maintaining a world class, best practice, high-quality and comprehensive e-governance system.

Seoul's government website maintains a user-friendly style. With clear block arrangement and appropriate length of first page, users can easily find the elements, content, or tools they need. The search tool on the first page also provides users an advanced channel to search for specific contents. Another tool "easy reads" links to a more simplified page style for people glancing at the most important things happening in the city. In sum, the website is designed in a friendly and clear style, which actually encourages use and interactions with the e-governance platform.

In addition to the high-level of usability, Seoul's government website features crucial factors that affect its e-governance level. First, ranked #1 in 100 cities in the world, Seoul's government website continues to act as a leading example of privacy protection and Internet security. Users are clearly notified about privacy issues while working with the website. Secondly, the website provides high-quality content that citizens are concerned with, including news, policies, government activities, and so on. Thirdly, services delivered online are also highly diverse, covering administrative applications to basic public services.

Most importantly, Seoul's government website features user-friendly and multi-channel citizen participation tools, which contribute to Seoul's being ranked #1 in the survey. Users can easily find accesses to several types of e-participation, including online petitions, debates, and citizen comment forums. In addition, on the first page, citizens can also directly send emails to the mayor. The website also indicates that citizens can use other social media to interact with the city government.

Helsinki

Helsinki was among the biggest "climbers" in the seventh Global E-Governance Survey. It went from #16 in the 2013-14 survey to #2 in the 2015-16 survey. Helsinki's high position is due largely to its success in the privacy (#3) and citizen and social engagement categories (#2).

The home page of the Helsinki website offers a good balance of detail and user friendliness. The entire home page does not require a large amount of page scrolling to reach the end; the headings and main content tabs are clear and create a useful template that is applied throughout the website. Helsinki's excellent usability is found throughout the site and its score is, overall, very high, affording it a position as #4 in the ranking.

In terms of privacy, the website has an information system description, which is legally mandated by Finnish law, and its e-services facility has a detailed privacy protection and information security page. The e-services facility also allows users to review and change their personal information. The website clearly states that user data is not collected for commercial use or shared with third party organizations.

Overall, privacy statements are clear and the intended use in terms of the specific kinds of data or the organization that is collecting it is stated explicitly. Statements on the use of cookies, notifications about changes in privacy policy, and details of how the information is stored are all available. In addition, there is a password protected e-services portal where private information can be accessed. Public information, meanwhile, is available throughout the website without need for a password.

Helsinki ranked #1 in citizen and social engagement. Public authorities are accessible through the website using interactive tools such as social media and comments platforms. There are contact emails for public officials and online noticeboards that post information relating to citizen participation in municipal activities. Importantly, the site also offers online forums that not only provide avenues for citizen discussion but also provide municipal responses to some of the issues that are raised.

Madrid

The city of Madrid has been a high performer in the Global E-Governance Survey for several years. After a brief dip in the 2013-14 survey, Madrid has regained its position near the top of the ranking thanks to high scores in services, citizen and social engagement, and good content organization and design. It is ranked #3. Several different kinds of municipal charges can be paid online. Madrid has a dedicated tax paying system online that users can utilize through a personal account. Other kinds of payments and fines can also be made online: municipal parking fees, fines, environmental and car control services, and social services. In addition, there is a registration page for accessing a series of municipal services.

Licenses and permit applications are well integrated with the personal online municipal accounts. Types of applications include commercial and residential licenses, workshop and zero emission parking permits, taxi permits, taxi ID cards, and licenses to extend or decrease the opening and closing hours of certain businesses. Not only can these applications be completed online, but applicants can follow the progress of the applications from the time the application is submitted through the steps leading to final approval.

Public officials and government departments can engage in communications through online forums. There is an area of the websites called "Debates" which includes ongoing public discussions between citizens and public officials. Some of the discussions are scheduled for specific dates and take place in real time through online chat platforms.

Hong Kong

The government website of Hong Kong is ranked #4 in the seventh Worldwide Digital Governance Survey. Though the rank declined from #3 in the previous survey, Hong Kong's actual score increased. The website is ranked #9 in Privacy and Security, #2 in Usability, #3 in Service Delivery, and #10 in Citizen and Social Engagement.

The website of Hong Kong is intended to provide citizens and other users a "one-stop" service platform, which is reflected in its high level of usability and service delivery. Contents are clearly categorized into different blocks on the main page, and key information such as budget reports and policy announcements is displayed fully. Thus, even though the length of the first page is limited, it still contains a large amount of information.

Multiple services can be accessed on the website, including business issues, administrative applications, citizenship applications, and others. The website also reflects government's concerns about services to non-citizens, who occupy a large portion of Hong Kong's population, in a specific section on the main page. Smart phone applications that access the website are also downloadable.

Other than the high level of usability and one-stop service delivery, Hong Kong's government website also shows average to high quality in other factors. Hong Kong performs well in protecting users' privacy and maintaining Internet security. Privacy policies and statements can be easily accessed by users, and personal data use is well-explained by the website.

Finally, the website also contains various platforms for citizen participation, such as online forums, efficient communications via e-mail, and social media platforms. With all these advanced elements on the website, Hong Kong acts as another leading example of digital government in Asia.

Prague

The Prague website is another consistently high performer in the Global E-Governance Survey, and in the seventh Survey it appears at #5 in the ranking. It has an effectively integrated approach to citizen participation. However, its high performance is mostly due to the way that it (1) addresses privacy concerns and (2) uses well-designed and useful information and material. It is ranked #2 and #4 on privacy policies and content respectively.

The site addresses questions of: what types of data are being collected? which organizations are collecting it? Not only is this level of data available, but users can access the privacy statement directly from all pages of the website. The intended use of the data is made clear and users are given the option to not have unsolicited material sent to them as a result of the data collected

Another area of best practice in the category of privacy and security is that privacy policy available on the website mentions that if the user clicks on a third party link placed on the city portal then they are in effect leaving the city portal and so the city privacy statement is not valid thereafter and the city cannot assume responsibility for third party actions.

Content-wise the site has excellent accessibility for public officials and departments using a searchable database of contact information. Many kinds of organizational statements are made clear and are easy to find including mission statements, minutes from meetings, and budgetary information. Performance information is published in the form of targets and benchmarks. Furthermore, these performance metrics are supplemented with information on the strategy being used to justify the choice of measurement instruments.

CHAPTER 11

Conclusion

There is marked importance in continuing the study of e-governance practices throughout the world in order to better understand what efforts are being taken to increase e-governance services across the components of Privacy/Security, Usability, Content, Service Delivery, and Citizen and Social Engagement. Our studies in 2003, 2005, 2007, 2009, 2011-12, 2013-14, and 2015-16 have produced findings that contribute to the e-governance literature and help to longitudinally measure developments on a macro and micro level for countries around the world. Previous research on government websites has focused primarily on e-governance at the federal, state, and local levels in the United States. This study seeks to expand upon this analysis and examine e-governance on a global scale. The continued effort of this research has been to map what advances are occurring among countries around the world in increasing their e-government capacities. Our research will continue as a longitudinal effort to evaluate digital governance in large municipalities throughout the world.

The 2015-16 study highlights advances made in each of the evaluated categories, and concludes that the results have shown that there has once again been increased attention paid to Usability and Content, and the need for further attention in the areas of Privacy/Security, Services, and Citizen and Social Engagement via municipal websites. The results largely mirror those of previous findings. Also, similar to our previous findings, Citizen and Social Engagement has recorded the lowest score among the five categories. Cities have not yet fully recognized the importance of involving and supporting citizen e-participation online.

However, there has been a rise in the average score in all five evaluation categories, which suggests that countries are taking more action to increase their capacities across all five categories even though they focus more noticeably on particular areas (i.e. content and usability). Among the five categories, governments have been steadily improving their e-governance scores longitudinally. Specifically, Content, Privacy/Security, Usability, Services, and Citizen and Social Engagement all increased slightly in 2015-16. This is evidence that cities have been making steady progress in building their e-governance capacities.

In mirroring best e-governance practices on the aggregate, continent level, governments should look especially to Oceania and Europe for best practices. Oceania was the highest ranked continent overall, and was followed by Europe. In looking at city examples of best e-governance, Seoul's model showcases many good practices. With regard to citizen e-participation channels, Seoul's model offers a multitude of tools, is easy to use and provides the best example of groundbreaking citizen and social engagement. With regard to Privacy/Security, the efforts of Prague have been exemplary in making their privacy policy comprehensive.

The site addresses what types of data are being collected and which organizations are collecting it. Further, users can access the privacy statement directly from all pages of the website. In addition, the intended use of the data is made clear and users are given the option to not have unsolicited material sent to them as a result of the data collected.

In addition, this survey has further taken note of the digital gap between OECD and non-OECD member countries in their average scores. It concludes that among all categories the scores of OECD and Non-OECD countries have increased, along with the overall average among these countries. These findings indicate the continued importance of international organizations, such as the UN and cities in advanced countries, in bridging the digital divide. Through showcasing best examples, the benefits of e-governance can be accurately communicated to nations in developing their e-governance efforts.

In many nations, especially those belonging to the non-OECD category, the digital divide may imply more than access to the Internet alone; this divide refers to access to basic infrastructure such as telephones, electricity, communications (Manoharan and Carrizales, 2010). Without such infrastructure, it becomes difficult for countries to increase their e-governance capacity to facilitate citizen use. We, therefore, recommend developing a comprehensive policy for bridging that divide. We advise that such a comprehensive policy should include capacity building for municipalities, including information infrastructure, content, applications and access for individuals, and educating residents with appropriate computer education.

The continued study of municipalities worldwide, with next evaluation planned in 2017, will further provide insights into the direction of e-governance and the performance of e-governance throughout regions of the world. Every region has examples of best practices for overall performance and in each specific e-governance category. As municipalities seek to increase their municipal website

performance, searching for models within their region is an opportunity to identify e-governance benchmarks. Those municipalities that serve as top perform-
ers in their respective regions can then look to the top-ranked cities throughout
the world for suggestions and advice on best practices and standards.

BIBLIOGRAPHY

Fudge, M. K., & Manoharan, A. (2013). Fear or Negligence? Contemporary Trends, Approaches and the Future of Online Privacy and Security Policies in US Cities. *IJeN,* 1(2), 22-37.

Giga Consulting. (2000). Scorecard Analysis of the New Jersey Department of Treasury. An unpublished report to the NJ Department of Treasury.

Holzer, M., Manoharan, A., & Van Ryzin, G. (2010). Global Cities on the Web: An Empirical Typology of Municipal Websites. *International Public Management Review.* 11(3), 104-121.

Holzer, M., Zheng, Y., Manoharan, A. & Shark, A. (2014). Digital Governance in Municipalities Worldwide (2013–14): Sixth Global E-Governance Survey: A Longitudinal Assessment of Municipal Websites throughout the World. *National Center for Public Performance, Rutgers University-Newark.*

Manoharan, A. (2013). A Study of the Determinants of County E-Government in the United States. *The American Review of Public Administration,* 43(2), 159-178.

Manoharan, A., & Carrizales, T. J. (2010). Technological Equity: An International Perspective of E-Government and Societal Divides. *Electronic Government, An International Journal,* 8(1), 73-84.

Moon, M. J. (2002). The Evolution of E-Government among Municipalities: Rhetoric or Reality? *Public Administration Review,* 62(4): 424-433.

Moon, M. Jae, and P. deLeon. (2001). Municipal Reinvention: Municipal Values and Diffusion among Municipalities. *Journal of Public Administration Research and Theory,* 11(3): 327-352.

Musso, J., Weare, C., & Hale, M. (2000). Designing Web Technologies for Local Governance Reform: Good Management or Good Democracy. *Political Communication,* 17(l): 1-19.

APPENDIX A: Cities and Websites

City	Country	Website
Addis Ababa	Ethiopia	www.addisababacity.gov.et/
Algiers	Algeria	N/A
Almaty	Kazakhstan	www.almaty.gov.kz/
Amman	Jordan	www.ammancity.gov.jo/
Amsterdam	Netherlands	www.iamsterdam.com
Athens	Greece	www.cityofathens.gr
Auckland	New Zealand	www.aucklandcouncil.govt.nz
Baku	Azerbaijan	www.baku-ih.gov.az/
Bangkok	Thailand	www.bangkok.go.th
Beirut	Lebanon	www.beirut.gov.lb/
Belgrade	Serbia	www.novibeograd.rs/
Berlin	Germany	www.berlin.de
Bishkek	Kyrgyzstan	www.meria.kg/
Bogotá	Colombia	www.bogota.gov.co
Bratislava	Slovakia	www.bratislava.sk/
Brussels	Belgium	www.be.brussels
Bucharest	Romania	www1.pmb.ro
Budapest	Hungary	www.budapest.hu/
Buenos Aires	Argentina	www.buenosaires.gob.ar
Cairo	Egypt	www.cairo.gov.eg
Caracas	Venezuela	www.caracas.gov.ve
Casablanca	Morocco	www.casablancacity.ma
Chisinau	Moldova	www.chisinau.md/
Colombo	Sri Lanka	www.cmc.lk/
Copenhagen	Denmark	www.kk.dk/
Damascus	Syria	www.damascus.gov.sy/
Delhi	India	www./delhi.gov.in/
Dhaka	Bangladesh	www.dncc.gov.bd (North Dhaka) & www.dhakasouthcity.gov.bd (South Dhaka)
Doha	Qatar	www.baladiya.gov.qa
Dubai	United Arab Emirates	www.dm.gov.ae/
Dublin	Ireland	www.dublincity.ie/
Gaza	Palestine	www.gaza-city.org/

City	Country	Website
Guatemala City	Guatemala	www.muniguate.com/
Guayaquil	Ecuador	www.guayaquil.gob.ec/
Helsinki	Finland	http://www.hel.fi/www/helsinki/en
Ho Chi Minh City	Viet Nam	www.hochiminhcity.gov.vn
Hong Kong	Hong Kong, China	www.gov.hk/
Istanbul	Turkey	www.ibb.gov.tr
Jakarta	Indonesia	www.jakarta.go.id/
Jerusalem	Israel	www.jerusalem.muni.il
Johannesburg	South Africa	www.joburg.org.za/
Karachi	Pakistan	www.kmc.gos.pk/
Kathmandu	Nepal	www.kathmandu.gov.np
Kiev	Ukraine	www.kyiv-obl.gov.ua
Kuala Lumpur	Malaysia	www.dbkl.gov.my
Lima	Peru	www.munlima.gob.pe/
Lisbon	Portugal	www.cm-lisboa.pt
Ljubljana	Slovenia	www.ljubljana.si/
London	United Kingdom	www.london.gov.uk
Luxembourg City	Luxembourg	www.vdl.lu/
Madrid	Spain	www.madrid.es
Manama	Bahrain	www.capital.gov.bh/
Manila	Philippines	www.manila.gov.ph
Mexico City	Mexico	www.cdmx.gob.mx
Rome	Italy	www.comune.roma.it
Minsk	Belarus	www.minsk.gov.by/ru/
Montevideo	Uruguay	www.montevideo.gub.uy
Moscow	Russia	www.mos.ru
Muscat	Oman	www.mm.gov.om/
New York	United States	www1.nyc.gov
Nicosia	Cyprus	www.nicosia.org.cy
Oslo	Norway	www.oslo.kommune.no/
Panama City	Panama	www.mupa.gob.pa
Paris	France	www.paris.fr

continued

City	Country	Website
Port Louis	Mauritius	www.mpl.intnet.mu/
Prague	Czech Republic	www.prague.eu/en
Riga	Latvia	www.riga.lv
Riyadh	Saudi Arabia	www.arriyadh.com/
San Fernando	Trinidad and Tobago	www.localgov.gov.tt/
San Jose	Costa Rica	www.msj.go.cr
San Juan	Puerto Rico	www.sanjuanciudadpatria.com/
San Salvador	El Salvador	www.sansalvador.gob.sv/
Sana'a	Yemen	www.sanaacity.com
Santiago	Chile	www.gobiernosantiago.cl/
Santo Domingo	Dominican Rep.	www.adn.gob.do/
São Paulo	Brazil	www.saopaulo.sp.gov.br
Sarajevo	Bosnia and Herzegovina	www.banjaluka.rs.ba
Seoul	South Korea	www.seoul.go.kr
Shanghai	China	www.shanghai.gov.cn
Singapore	Singapore	www.gov.sg/
Skopje	Macedonia	www.skopje.gov.mk/
Sofia	Bulgaria	www.sofia.bg/
Stockholm	Sweden	www.stockholm.se
Sydney	Australia	www.cityofsydney.nsw.gov.au
Taipei	Taiwan	www.ntpc.gov.tw/
Tallinn	Estonia	www.tallinn.ee/
Tashkent	Uzbekistan	www.tashkent.uz/
Tbilisi	Georgia	www.tbilisi.gov.ge/
Tehran	Iran	www.tehran.ir
Tirana	Albania	www.tirana.gov.al
Tokyo	Japan	www.metro.tokyo.jp/
Toronto	Canada	www1.toronto.ca/
Tunis	Tunisia	www.commune-tunis.gov.tn
Ulaanbaatar	Mongolia	www.ulaanbaatar.mn
Vienna	Austria	www.wien.gv.at/
Vilnius	Lithuania	www.vilnius.lt
Warsaw	Poland	www.um.warszawa.pl
Yerevan	Armenia	www.yerevan.am/am/
Zagreb	Croatia	www.zagreb.hr
Zurich	Switzerland	www.stadt-zuerich.ch

APPENDIX B: E-Governance Performance Measures

Privacy/Security	
1-2. A privacy or security statement/ policy	12. Secure server
3-6. Data collection	13. Use of "cookies" or "Web Beacons"
7. Option to have personal information used	14. Notification of privacy policy
8. Third party disclosures	15. Contact or e-mail address for inquiries
9. Ability to review personal data records	16. Public information through a restricted area
10. Managerial measures	17. Access to nonpublic information for employees
11. Use of encryption	18. Use of digital signatures
Usability	
19-20. Homepage, page length.	25-27. Font Color
21. Targeted audience	30-31. Forms
22-23. Navigation Bar	32-37. Search tool
24. Site map	38. Update of website
Content	
39. Information about the location of offices	49. GIS capabilities
40. Listing of external links	50. Emergency management or alert mechanism
41. Contact information	51-52. Disability access
42. Minutes of public	53. Wireless technology
43. City code and regulations	54. Access in more than one language
44. City charter and policy priority	55-56. Human resources information
45. Mission statements	57. Calendar of events
46. Budget information	58. Downloadable documents
47-48. Documents, reports, or books (publications)	

continued

Service	
59-61. Pay utilities, taxes, fines	70-71. Bulletin board about civil applications
62. Apply for permits	72. FAQ
63. Online tracking system	73. Request information
64-65. Apply for licenses	74. Customize the main city homepage
66. E-procurement	75. Access private information online
67. Property assessments	76. Purchase tickets
68. Searchable databases	77. Webmaster response
69. Complaints	78. Report violations of administrative laws and regulations
Citizen and Social Engagement	
79-80. Comments or feedback	90-91. Online survey/ polls
81-83. Newsletter	92. Synchronous video
84. Online bulletin board or chat capabilities	93-94. Citizen satisfaction survey
85-87. Online discussion forum on policy issues	95. Online decision-making
88-89. Scheduled e-meetings for discussion	96-104. Performance measures, standards, or benchmarks

ABOUT THE AUTHORS

DR. MARC HOLZER, University Professor and Former Dean of the Rutgers School of Public Affairs and Administration, is a leading expert in performance measurement, public management and e-governance. He is the founder and director of the National Center for Public Performance, a research and public service organization devoted to improving performance in the public sector. He also developed the E-Governance Institute, created to explore the on-going impact of the Internet and other information technologies on the productivity and performance of the public sector, and how e-government fosters new and deeper citizen involvement within the governing process. Dr. Holzer's recent publications include *Performance Measurement; Citizen-Driven Government Performance; the Public Productivity Handbook; Restoring Trust in Government: The Potential of Digital Citizen Participation, and Building Good Governance: Reforms in Seoul.* He has published well over one hundred books, monographs, chapters and articles. He is a Fellow of the National Academy of Public Administration and of the World Academy of Productivity Science. He is a Past President of the American Society for Public Administration (ASPA) and is a recipient of several national and international awards in the field, including the ASPA Dwight Waldo Award for outstanding contributions to the professional literature of public administration over an extended career (2013); the Distinguished Research Award from the Network of Schools of Public Policy, Affairs, and Administration (NASPAA) and the American Society for Public Administration (2009); the Sweeney Academic Award from the International City Management Association (2005); the Donald Stone National ASPA Achievement Award (1994); and the William and Frederick Mosher Award for Best Article by an Academician Appearing in the *Public Administration Review* (2001). He directs the Memoranda of Understanding between ASPA and the United Nations Division of Public Administration and Public Economics, the Korean Association of Public Administration, the Chinese Public Administration Society, and the European Group on Public Administration. He founded the Northeast Conference on Public Administration and ASPA Sections on Korea, China and Humanities/Arts.

DR. AROON P. MANOHARAN is an Associate Professor in the John W. McCormack Graduate School of Policy and Global Studies at the University of Massachusetts, Boston. He is also the Director of the Global Comparative Master of Public Administration (MPA) program. His research interests include e-governance, performance measurement and reporting, strategic planning, public management, and comparative public administration. He holds an MPA from the Kansas State University and a Ph.D. from the School of Public Affairs and Administration, Rutgers University-Newark. His research employs an international comparative focus, and he has participated in e-government projects in Prague (Czech Republic), Sofia (Bulgaria), and Cape Town (South Africa). Dr. Manoharan's research has been published in the *American Review of Public Administration, State and Local Government Review, Public Administration Quarterly, Journal of Public Affairs Education, International Journal of Public Sector Management, International Journal of Public Administration, International Journal of Organization Theory and Behavior, and International Public Management Review.* His book *E-Government and Websites: A Public Solutions Handbook,* offers a citizen-centric perspective of e-governance, with key suggestions for practitioners. In addition to conference presentations and invited lectures, he currently serves as peer reviewer for several scholarly publications.

www.ingramcontent.com/pod-product-compliance
Lightning Source LLC
Chambersburg PA
CBHW060154290526
45789CB00003B/1030